The MARTIAL ARTS Kettlebell CONNECTION

STRENGTH-BUILDING EXERCISES FOR SUPERIOR RESULTS

JOHN SPEZZANO

BLACK BELT PRESENTS

The MARTIAL ARTS Kettlebell CONNECTION

STRENGTH-BUILDING EXERCISES FOR SUPERIOR RESULTS

JOHN SPEZZANO

Edited by Sarah Dzida, Cassandra Harris and Jeannine Santiago
Graphic Design by John Bodine and Val Echavarria
Photographs by Thomas Sanders

Black Belt Books, Valencia CA 91355

First Printing 2010

Printed in South Korea

Library of Congress Number: 2010938182
ISBN-10: 0-89750-193-4
ISBN-13: 978-0-89750-193-4

For information about permission to reproduce selections from this book, write Black Belt Books, 24900 Anza Dr. Unit E Valencia, CA. 91355

For information about bulk/wholesale purchases, please contact 1 (800) 423-2874 ext. 1633

WARNING

This book is presented only as a means of preserving a unique aspect of the heritage of the martial arts. Neither Ohara Publications nor the author makes any representation, warranty or guarantee that the techniques described or illustrated in this book will be safe or effective in any self-defense situation or otherwise. You may be injured if you apply or train in the techniques illustrated in this book and neither Ohara Publications nor the author is responsible for any such injury that may result. It is essential that you consult a physician regarding whether or not to attempt any technique described in this book. Specific self-defense responses illustrated in this book may not be justified in any particular situation in view of all of the circumstances or under applicable federal, state or local law. Neither Ohara Publications nor the author makes any representation or warranty regarding the legality or appropriateness of any technique mentioned in this book.

ACKNOWLEDGMENTS

Without my parents, I wouldn't be writing this book. They instilled in me a hunger to learn and gave me the freedom to live life my way, even when they disagreed with my course. Guro Dan Inosanto is undeniably my father in martial arts. He is the consummate student and teacher. Without his example, I would have no compass. Many thanks also go to Sarah Dzida, my unbelievably patient editor who carried me along through the deceptively challenging editing process. Dr. Mark Cheng, my simultaneous brother, martial arts student and kettlebell coach, has been a constant source of information and inspiration. Mark and Lisa Twight from Gym Jones, are friends like few others. Finally of course my wife, Suzanne, without her support, none of what I do would get done.

TABLE OF CONTENTS

ABOUT THE AUTHOR

John Spezzano has spent nearly 30 years training and teaching traditional and cutting-edge martial arts. Spezzano was a staff instructor at the Inosanto Academy of Martial Arts in Los Angeles from 1995 to 2009 where he taught weekly Philippine martial arts classes as well as classes with mixed curricula drawn from multiple martial arts. He is a full instructor in Philippine martial arts and *jeet kune do* under Dan Inosanto as well as a certified instructor of *wing chun* under Francis Fong. Spezzano also holds instructor-level rank in *muay Thai* under Chai Sirisute, *boxe française savate* under Nicolas Saignac and satria fighting arts under Steve Benitez. Additionally, Spezzano is a defensive-tactics instructor for Operational Skills Group, which caters to various military and law-enforcement agencies around the country. Outside the martial arts and defensive-tactics worlds, Spezzano is an RKC (Russian kettlebell certified) instructor under Pavel Tsatsouline. Spezzano trains regularly with RKC team leader Dr. Mark Cheng, who is on the front line of hard-style kettlebell instruction.

Spezzano runs the muay Thai and kettlebell programs for Five Star Martial Arts in Los Angeles and holds the rank of purple belt under Shawn Williams, the owner of Five Star who is also a Renzo Gracie black belt. When he's not teaching muay Thai or kettlebells at Five Star or conducting martial arts seminars around the United States and Europe, Spezzano trains private clients in Los Angeles. To learn more, visit pacificcoast-martialarts.com and hollywoodkettlebells.com.

CHAPTER 1

Movement, Mind-set and Balance

Martial arts is at best a vague term encompassing vast and varied approaches to combat from cultures around the globe. Many martial arts focus on striking, some emphasize ground control and submission techniques, and others let their weaponry do the talking. If you're into Brazilian *jiu-jitsu*, you might be wondering how the same kettlebell exercises that improve your training and performance will help your buddy who trains in *muay Thai*. Or, if you're a *kali* man, you might not believe a grappler's strength and conditioning regimen could possibly work to improve your stick fighting. Believe it. Whether you swing a stick or shoot a double-leg takedown, if you can't move properly as a martial artist, then you're up the creek. The simple fact is that all combat sports revolve around unimpeded, strong and explosive movements, and hard-style kettlebell training strikes a balance between those attributes.

Balance is not a new concept. The *yin-yang* symbol, synonymous with martial arts and arguably the most recognizable Asian symbol in existence, epitomizes the idea of blending opposites to create a balanced whole. Hard-style kettlebell training incorporates this idea with two polar-opposite categories of exercise: ballistics and grinds. Ballistic exercises use momentum to move the kettlebell, while grinds are performed from a standstill. Together, these two types of kettlebell exercises improve both ends of the movement spectrum: the explosive and the methodical. The sharp, directed motion of ballistic exercises such as the Two-Handed Swing and the Snatch give near-instant gains in cardio, strength and flexibility. Conversely, grinds such as the Turkish Get Up and the Military Press use compromised positions to develop raw power and strength at odd angles, which are outstanding attributes for any martial artist. If the methodical is not balanced with the explosive, something will suffer: the body, the results or both.

You know from your martial arts training that the mind and the body are another example of yin and yang. They are opposites yet undeniably linked. Nothing the mind imagines can be accomplished physically without the body. Similarly, the body will not push onward in the face of likely defeat without the urging of a determined mind. The two must coexist, and if they work well together, they will combine to make your fighting spirit greater than it would be otherwise. The combination of mind and body is essential for success in martial arts when you face a tough opponent. It's also vital in hard-style kettlebells when doubt creeps into your head, making you second-guess your ability to push your training to the next level. A balanced strong mind and body will help you in the challenges of everyday life, as well.

The Bottoms-Up Windmill is a grind that requires maximum control over the kettlebell.

The One-Handed Swing With Vertical Flip is a challenging ballistic that is only successfully completed with maximum explosion of the hips and simultaneous control and timing of the kettlebell.

The *yin-yang* symbol epitomizes the simultaneous use of opposites to balance the whole.

There are literally hundreds of exercises you can perform with the kettlebell. The limit is, quite truly, your imagination. Through hundreds and then thousands and then tens of thousands of repetitions, you will comprehend the exercises on a physical and, hopefully, cellular level. Each time you touch the handle of the kettlebell, you will know how to move it with less conscious thought every time. After that, it's up to you to challenge yourself. Start with the intentionally methodical and detailed introduction to the exercises in this book. Then complete the recommended exercise routines. Finally, feel free to make up your own.

Don't rush! The patience and attention to detail required for all the kettlebell exercises you are about to learn means your mind needs to be focused and wrapped around your training. You have to simultaneously train hard *and* safe, so don't zone out. Pay attention to what you're doing, and be certain to get your ego out of the way. Recognize that the kettlebell is the tool, but that quality reps, the only type worth doing, are the result of a mentally focused effort. Only precise movement patterns through proper loading procedures will allow you to safely and rapidly reach your desired strength and conditioning goals. Focus on the details of the exercises, and use a kettlebell of appropriate size for your strength and experience. Do not rush yourself through the learning process.

Finally, just like martial arts training, realize that true progress depends on the perfection of your form for all the exercises, not just the ones you are naturally good at. Keep your mind in the game, and you will get the results you desire. Once the results start appearing, don't get lazy. Maintain and increase your attention to detail during your training. Always go the extra mile in your training, but realize it is your *mind* and its commitment to the physical task at hand that makes the body's success possible. A strong mental approach will allow you to succeed at the physical challenges you give yourself. In so doing, your fighting spirit will grow strong. You will come to know yourself better and realize there is nothing you cannot do. This is the true essence of martial arts—self-discovery.

Kettlebell Training Benefits

1. **Functional Strength:**
   Olympic lifters use explosive movement to put big weight overhead, while powerlifters grind out maximum poundage with no momentum. Both these approaches use the body as a whole to move the weight. Hard-style kettlebell training does the same. Why is that a big deal? Combat movements are always full-body movements. Think about the simple act of punching: The force of the punch is generated not by your arm's movement but by the movement of your entire body.

2. **Full-Body Stability:**
   It's like putting on a protective outer shield because as the great Rocky Balboa says, "In fighting, it ain't about how hard you hit, it's about how hard you can get hit and keep moving forward!" (I love that scene!) I'm not saying that taking your opponent's best shot should be your go-to defensive move. I'm just saying that having the capability to withstand punishment is yet another ace up your sleeve.

3. **Explosiveness:**
   Make a strong movement crisp and staccato and you have explosiveness. The ability to move your hips explosively is arguably the core of countless martial arts movements—kicks, throws, punches. Explosive movement developed through hard-style kettlebell training will put force behind your speed.

4. **Cardiovascular Conditioning:**
   My teacher Dan Inosanto often says, "Be able to go 15 rounds . . . but don't go 15 rounds." Strength and cardiovascular capacity are developed simultaneously with ballistic kettlebell exercises. The "burst interval" nature of ballistics directly relates to the ebb and flow of martial arts competition. This is the type of cardiovascular conditioning you will develop with the kettlebell.

5. **Flexibility:**
   The conventional understanding of flexibility is being able to comfortably touch your toes or kick someone in the head. Don't get me wrong. Hard-style kettlebells will also help with this, but flexibility simply means that you move without restriction. Less restriction allows your body to use more efficient movement. More efficient movement means better use of all your other attributes whether in training or competition. Hard-style training will help eliminate restricted movement and allow your attributes to come through all on their own.

CHAPTER 2

Foundational Exercises

If you search for "kettlebell exercises" on the Internet, 0.24 seconds later you will have more than 2 million results at your fingertips. I can guarantee that you don't need that much kettlebell material to get the results you want. Instead, you just need to pick the right exercises and do them properly.

Let's get something out of the way right now—I can't tell you how many times I've heard people say, "Kettlebells hurt my back," or something equally ridiculous. This common belief is more accurately blamed on improper execution of an exercise. In a nutshell, kettlebells don't hurt your back. Your incorrect movement and alignment will. So pay attention and do the exercises properly!

If your goal is to use kettlebells with the express intention of greatly improving your martial arts training and performance, then what exercises should you do and why? First and foremost, develop a knowledge base of foundational movement patterns and fundamental exercises such as the Face-the-Wall Squat, the Hard-Style Lock, the Deadlift, the Two-Handed Swing and the Turkish Get Up. This short list of exercises will safely teach you how to properly load the human body as well as how to move under that load with stability (strength and control) both explosively quick and methodically slow. Stability instantly reduces your risk of injury and will also deliver greater results to your martial arts training and performance.

THE FACE-THE-WALL SQUAT

I know you're jonesing to start moving iron, but it's essential we lay down a stable foundation so you're not the next person I hear blame kettlebells for some self-inflicted injury. In our Los Angeles group, we always begin practice without weight in hand because we believe that moving the load before you can move your own body weight safely is an injury waiting to happen. So this is how you'll get started with the simple but challenging Face-the-Wall Squat.

Children innately squat with their back in a safe position, while most adults pick something up off the ground by bending at the waist. While adults have forgotten they have knees and constantly put their lower back at risk of injury, young children do not. Add time and laziness to the equation and you get a fiercely ingrained movement pattern that most adults use to squat, which is really not a squat at all. Instead, it's just an awkward bend and people wonder how they hurt their backs ... but I digress.

It is vital to understand how to properly load the human frame for lifting weight. Merely bending over at the waist is not a safe method to do so. To start, your back cannot round; it must stay flat. At the same time, your chest needs to stay as upright as possible. The more your chest faces the ground, the more you are likely to transfer the weight to your lower back and risk injury. A wrestler doesn't shoot a double-leg takedown by bending at the waist. A muay Thai fighter doesn't round his back looking at the floor while in the clinch. Every jiu-jitsu student knows good posture is step No. 1 to passing the guard. Outside of martial arts training and competition, good posture is essential to strength-train safely and injury free and also quite helpful in everyday chores.

The Face-the-Wall Squat is step No. 1 in your reprogramming. Your squat pattern needs be trained so you squat without pushing your knees forward past your toes while at the same time keeping your chest tall. This movement pattern is a one-stop shop for fixing bad squat form. So with that in mind, find a wall!

The Face-the-Wall Squat

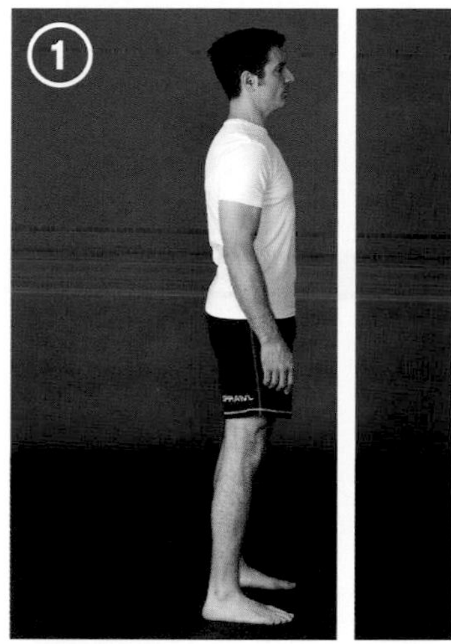

1. Stand facing a wall from about six inches away with your feet shoulder-width apart and parallel.

2. Pull your butt back and down as far as you can go while keeping your chest tall and not letting your knees push forward past your toes. Hold at the bottom for a beat.

3. Return to your original standing position. Repeat steps one through three for three sets of 10 reps. Get plenty of rest in between sets if you need it.

You have likely noticed that performing this exercise is not as simple as it sounds. If you do it incorrectly, you will hit your knees or your head against the wall. These bumps are what I commonly refer to as "self-correcting" errors because completing the exercise is impossible unless done correctly. It's always safest to receive such corrective feedback with no weight overhead.

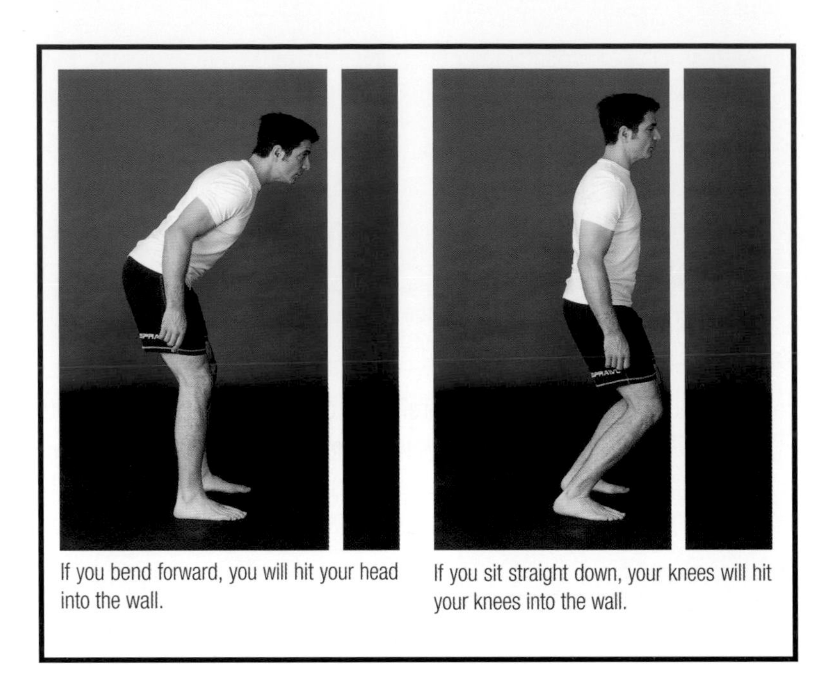

If you bend forward, you will hit your head into the wall.

If you sit straight down, your knees will hit your knees into the wall.

You probably felt your back muscles waking up as you forced them to pull your chest tall. This is to be expected because the Face-the-Wall Squat cannot be executed with spinal flexibility alone. The Face-the-Wall Squat also requires back *strength.* It is your back strength that pulls your chest vertically in line with the wall and allows you to complete the movement. For now, while your back strength develops, just focus on pulling your butt back and down as low as you can. If you can pull yourself low enough to get your thighs parallel to the ground at the bottom, great. If you can't, then just get as low as you can, making sure you track your toes in line with your knees while pulling your butt back and down. In addition to being a challenging body-weight exercise, this simultaneous back-and-down motion will transfer directly to any level-changing kettlebell exercise, such as a Two-Handed Swing. It will also help any martial arts training that requires a level change—takedowns and throws come to mind.

THE HARD-STYLE LOCK

Now that you understand the Face-the-Wall Squat, your next building block is the Hard-Style Lock. This five-point sequence starts at the heels and works upward to the knees, glutes, abdominals and lats—essentially the entire body. The "lock" in the name refers to the deliberate full-body tension that is generated at each of the five points.

The Hard-Style Lock is performed during every hard-style kettlebell exercise that makes use of standing posture. This full-body tension is essential for the optimal execution of hard-style exercises. Tension makes overhead stabilization of weight more secure, unlike when your muscles are relaxed. Also, the full-body tension forces your body to activate large numbers of major muscle groups, which means you'll be getting superior results and performance on the mat in record time.

When learning the upcoming Hard-Style Lock sequence, feel free to separate the steps because it's important to get the concept and execution ingrained fully. Once you understand the movement though, you'll want to force your body to hit all five parts of the sequence simultaneously.

The five-point sequence is as follows:

1. **Heels:** With your feet shoulder-width apart and strictly parallel, come to a standing position from a Face-the-Wall Squat (no wall necessary). Drive your weight into the ground through your heels, not your toes. Loading your heels this way puts your skeleton into direct contact with the ground, taking unnecessary joints and musculature out of the equation. This increased efficiency means your skeleton supports the kettlebell rather than your musculature. It also optimizes your power delivery to move the bell.
2. **Knees:** I know people don't do it often, but Point 2 of the Hard-Style Lock is to fully straighten your knees. Do it gradually at first, but be sure to straighten your legs fully by pushing the backs of your knees to an area somewhere behind you. Some people prefer the cue of imagining they are pulling the kneecaps up to the hips. Whichever cue you prefer, just lock your knees straight. Once the knees are locked, you are again using your musculature to make the skeleton carry external weight. In addition to using your skeleton to support the weight, fully locking the knees will also help to more completely recruit the glutes to lend a hand in the lift, as you'll see in a moment.
3. **Glutes:** A well-executed Point 2 will help you grasp Point 3. While performing Point 2, clench your glutes for all they're worth. Hold the tension for a few beats and get a sense of how hard and thoroughly you can fire them. Good, relax for a second. Now with your knees unlocked and legs noticeably bent, fire your glutes as hard as you did a moment ago. The difference in your ability to use your glutes with your knees unlocked should be shockingly apparent. This is a big deal because not using the glutes is likely a large contributing factor to why people hurt their back and blame the kettlebell. When your glutes are not fully engaged, your lower back has to pick up the slack. Locking your knees will help you clench your glutes, making glute recruitment much easier to achieve. Once your glutes are engaged, they will take the load rather than placing it on the lower back—where it doesn't belong in the first place. The more work your glutes can do, the better.
4. **Abs:** Your lower back is sandwiched between your abdominals and your glutes. Whereas your clenched glutes from Point 3 protect your lower back from below, your abs protect your lower back from above. If you fire your abs with everything you've got, you will not be able to lean backward and put undue stress on your lower back. Just like locking the knees helps fire the glutes with no additional thought, exhaling a short, staccato breath with your tongue on the roof of your mouth will help you subconsciously employ your abs. (Think of it as essentially a standing crunch when you reach the fully upright position.) Give it a try by doing two strong exhales. Do the first one shortly and crisply with your tongue on the roof of your mouth. Do the second exhale slowly without your tongue in position. See the difference for yourself. Isolate this breath exercise from the previous points for now so you can feel the difference in the abs, then synchronize it as you work these four parts of the Hard-Style Lock in tandem.
5. **Lats:** The lats are called the "wing" muscles and are the largest muscles of the back. They flare out from the lower spine like wings, cover the majority of your back and end underneath your armpits. From a strictly muscular standpoint, their job is to pull the arm downward. But the lats can help a lot when moving weight in an explosive and controlled fashion. In particular, lats generate specific shoulder stability and overall core stability, which are essential characteristics when moving weight. The lats help you keep the shoulders "packed" or secure in their sockets. They also maintain symmetry in the torso even when the upper body is loaded asymmetrically on only one side. Clenching your fists and flexing every muscle in your arms will garner further full-body tension.

These five points make up the Hard-Style Lock and should be performed simultaneously after rising up from a Face-the-Wall Squat or any kettlebell exercise that uses a squatting movement. So this means you'll be doing it *a lot*.

When first learning the Hard-Style Lock, feel free to break the sequence into its component parts and add steps incrementally as you work your way through some squats to warm up. For example, do 10 squats and come up, finishing with Point 1: Drive your heels into the ground. Then do 10 more squats and finish up by driving your heels down and locking your knees. Then add the glutes, abs and lats in succession until you are rising up from your squats and hitting all five points of the Hard-Style Lock at the top on every rep. When performed properly, the Hard-Style Lock will generate full-body tension through the use of the legs, glutes, abs and lats. This tension will give you a stable base for every kettlebell exercise that finds itself in the standing position, thereby increasing your ability to train safely.

The Hard-Style Lock

1. Pull yourself down into a good squat.

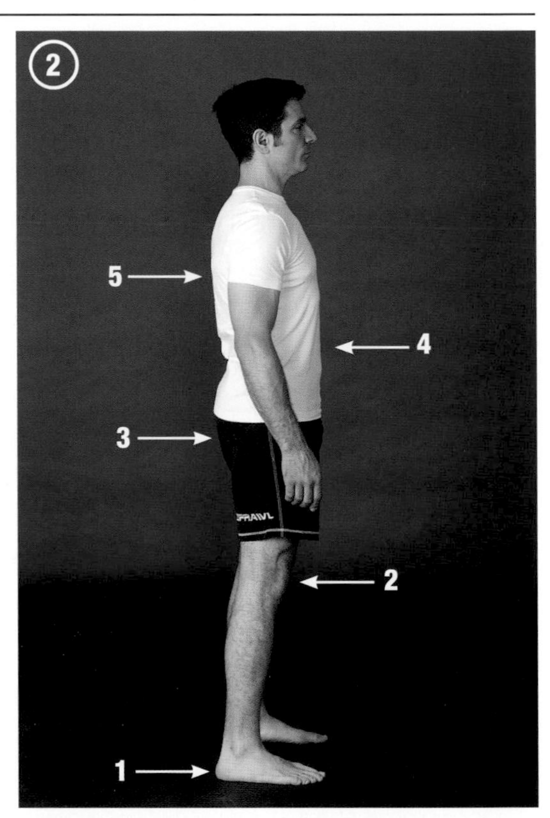

2. Rise up and hit all five points of the Hard-Style Lock simultaneously.

Good Posture, Bad Posture

Whether on the mat training, or going about daily life, people spend a lot of time typically oblivious to their posture. Sitting at desks and driving cars, not to mention using a protective stance so as not to be kicked, punched or taken down in training, people and martial artists often find themselves pushing their shoulders and head forward. This is not good posture. Good posture forms a straight line that is perpendicular to the ground and intersects with your ankle, knee, hip, shoulder and ear. It is necessary when training to round your shoulders and tuck your chin, but doing so when not training compromises your posture and builds bad habits. The Hard-Style Lock generates a physical familiarity with good posture. Be sure when you practice your Hard-Style Lock that you finish with proper alignment of the ankle, knee, hip, shoulder and ear.

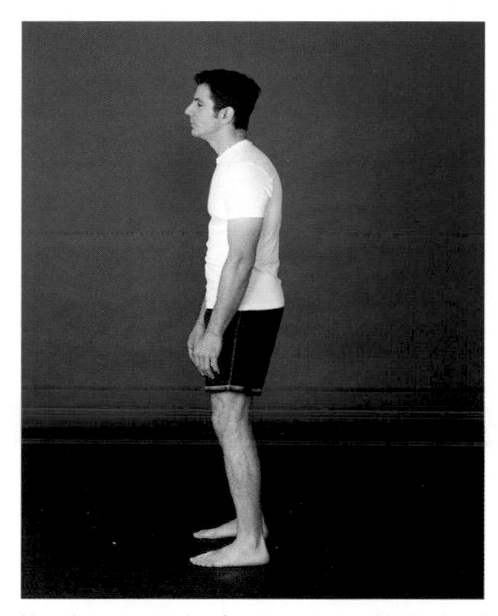

Here is an example of poor posture with the head "chicken necking" forward and the shoulders rounded.

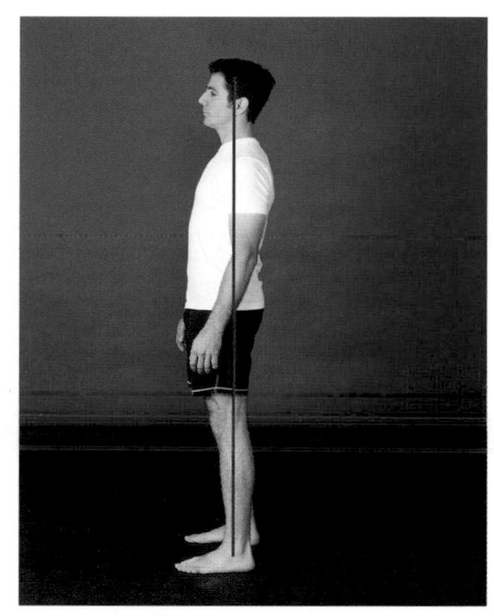

Here is an example of good posture with the ankle, knee, hip, shoulder and ear in line.

THE DEADLIFT

You now have the Face-the-Wall Squat and Hard-Style Lock mastered, and that means you're ready to start handling the iron. The Deadlift is the best way to safely introduce you to the kettlebell and is your key to linking the Face-the-Wall Squat and the full-body tension of the Hard-Style Lock with the iron itself.

In addition to perfecting proper movement patterns for other kettlebell exercises, the Deadlift is outstanding practice for realistic lifting in daily life. You're going to use a light but versatile size kettlebell, the 16 kg for the gents and the 8 kg for the ladies, to facilitate efficient training that avoids injury. These are good starting weights for most people because they are big enough to be physically challenging but small enough for the beginner to use safely. Also, as your skill increases, these size kettlebells will remain useful in future training. They will not gather dust.

Some people are scared of the Deadlift because of its name. However, the name only implies that the weight is lifted off the ground from a standstill. The Deadlift won't kill you and is arguably the most practical lift in existence, no matter your choice of training regimen. Don't be scared of this lift, folks, just do it right! Simply put, the Deadlift is a Face-the-Wall Squat with a kettlebell in hand and a Hard-Style Lock at the top. Aside from the presence of the kettlebell, nothing changes from the movement patterns you've already learned. So let's start moving some kettlebells!

Now that you are moving weight around, it's vital to focus on footwear and shoulder safety. Barefoot training is the preferred method for training hard-style kettlebells. The toes spread naturally when barefoot, and this greater physical contact with the ground heightens your sensitivity to balance. If you can't train barefoot, wear flat-soled shoes only. No running shoes. The raised heel of a running shoe shifts your weight forward, and that counteracts all the good work you did when learning the Face-the-Wall Squat and the Hard-Style Lock.

THE DEADLIFT

In regards to shoulder safety, the biggest issue is that most people have grown far too accustomed to shrugging. They reach for items in the cupboard by doing so and lift objects from the ground in the same manner. It's not a good habit. Just think about what a shrug implies: indecision and uncertainty. Are those the qualities of a fighter who is going to win his match? I don't think so! Seriously though, shrugging predisposes you to increased risk of shoulder, collarbone and neck injury. When you perform

Using the Deadlift for picking objects up in everyday life is a great idea. Skiers joke about lifting with their back to save their legs for skiing. It's hilarious until you hurt yourself.

the fifth and final step of the Hard-Style Lock, think about pushing your fingertips down the outsides of your quads and "shutting" your armpits by pinning your upper arms to your rib cage. Make sure your shoulders are pushing back and down into the sockets. All these motions should create a "packing" effect, which you learned about in Point 5 of the Hard-Style Lock. When weight is involved, this packed shoulder position is preferably employed immediately after putting your hands on the kettlebell handle rather than when you just hit the top of your Hard-Style Lock. Keep it all in mind: When you get tired and your lats relax, you will very likely encourage shoulder and collarbone issues. I am speaking from experience; one bad rep a few years back led to months of collarbone pain that proved very difficult to deal with. Learn from my mistake folks, use your lats.

The Deadlift

Gentlemen: 16 kg / Ladies: 8 kg

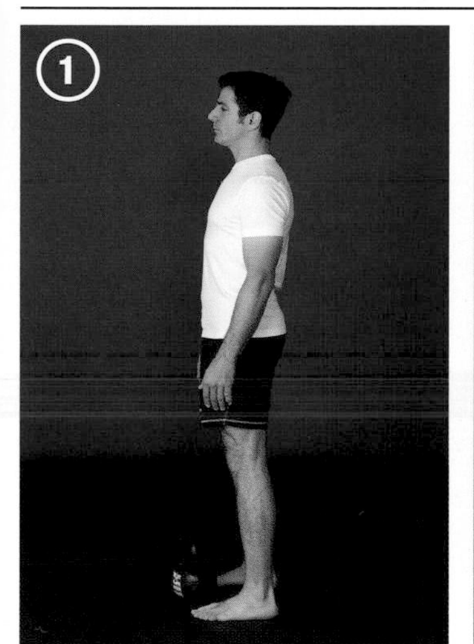

1. Stand directly over the kettlebell so you can see the handle just in front of your stomach.

2. Pull yourself back and down in pristine Face-the-Wall-Squat fashion. Make sure your body weight stays loaded into your heels. Keep your chest tall and facing forward rather than at the floor. Get a firm grip on the kettlebell with both hands. Fire your lats as soon as you grip the bell to keep those shoulders safe.

3. While maintaining your two-handed grip on the kettlebell, drive your heels into the ground and come to a standing finish in a crisp Hard-Style Lock. Be sure to hit all five points of the Hard-Style Lock—heels, knees, glutes, abs and lats. Just like you generated tension throughout your arms by clenching your fists without weight, crush the handle now to generate that same tension, which will also increase your grip strength. Hold the standing position for a three-count to confirm you are using the true full-body tension from the Hard-Style Lock.

4. Lower the bell to the ground by pulling your butt back and down in the same Face-the-Wall-Squat manner. (If lack of flexibility keeps you from touching the bell to the ground with every rep, lower yourself at least enough so your forearms touch your inner thighs.) Once the bell hits bottom, repeat the sequence for a set of 10 repetitions.

Focus maximum attention to detail on the descending squat pattern. Also, really hold onto that true full-body tension via a solid Hard-Style Lock at the end of the rise. Doing so will surprise you with the amount of physical output required for such a simple-looking exercise. Take sufficient rest to fully recover, then do two more sets of 10 repetitions to get an initial feel for the exercise. Hundreds more reps are needed for mastery.

Do not grab the handle like this.

Limited Flexibility

If you have flexibility issues that preclude you from getting low enough to even grasp the bell with good form, here is a solution. Lower yourself to the kettlebell as best you can. Obtain your grip on the bell and evaluate your posture. If it bears no resemblance to the bottom of your Face-the-Wall Squat—your chest is facing the ground, your back is rounded or your knees are forward of your toes—you need to fine-tune it a bit before actually executing the lift. Maintain your grip, pause at the bottom and use your grip to lever against the weight of the kettlebell. Doing so will help you pull your butt lower to the ground while sitting back on your heels. Be sure your back is flat. No rounding! Also, be sure your shoulders are pulled back and down into the socket by firing your lats. Once you have checked those points off the list, execute the Deadlift.

If you can't squat to the kettlebell with good form, bend at the hips and grab the handle.

Use the weight of the bell on the ground to pull yourself down into a good squat position before executing the exercise.

The Program Minimum

Now that the Face-the-Wall Squat, Hard-Style Lock and Deadlift have educated your mind and body on how to properly move weight, you can actually start moving some kettlebells. The Deadlift taught you the mechanics of proper lifting, which will help you accomplish the Program Minimum.

The Program Minimum is shorthand for the two most important hard-style exercises: the Two-Handed Swing and the Turkish Get Up. These two exercises are polar opposites of each other. They work in complementary fashion, following a balanced yin-yang training methodology by blending ballistic and grind exercises. The Two-Handed Swing adds explosive motion to the Deadlift and becomes the first and most important step in hard-style ballistic training. The Two-Handed Swing is the most significant ballistic exercise because it teaches the most important part of the ballistic movement pattern that you will use again and again in your hard-style kettlebell training. That movement is lower-body explosiveness that comes from thrusting your hips forward. In your martial arts training, you'll find this explosiveness helpful for speeding up striking attacks and throwing techniques. The Turkish Get Up is the most important grind exercise because it requires maximum strength and mobility at odd angles. It compliments any other exercise or combative skill that needs simultaneous full-body strength with shoulder and hip mobility and stability at the same time. Any kind of clinch work or ground fighting comes to mind.

The Program Minimum might seem basic, but it is the foundation of the hard-style system of training. It builds attributes such as speed, strength and range of motion, which are useful in any martial arts pursuit. Don't be seduced by a desire to juggle kettlebells simply because your YouTube clip will look cool. You are not moving bells as an end in itself but rather as a means to improve your martial arts performance. So let's finish laying the foundation by gaining a thorough understanding of the Program Minimum. These two exercises alone will help you make tremendous progress in strength, stability, range of motion, explosiveness and cardiovascular conditioning, all of which are vital attributes for any martial artist.

THE TWO-HANDED SWING

The Two-Handed Swing transforms the Deadlift into the quintessential hard-style ballistic exercise. It is also a perfect example of the phrase "simple but not easy." A Two-Handed Swing simply moves the bell at arm's length from between your legs to out in front of your chest, then repeats. How hard can that be? The ease of the Two-Handed Swing can be visually misleading. While it looks simple, it is building leg strength, hip explosiveness and grip strength, which are definitely necessary qualities for any martial artist. For your cardio benefits, it is also spiking your heart rate within 30 seconds of training. This could be useful in the opening seconds of any match when your excitement gets the better of you or in the last round when you need some extra gas in the tank.

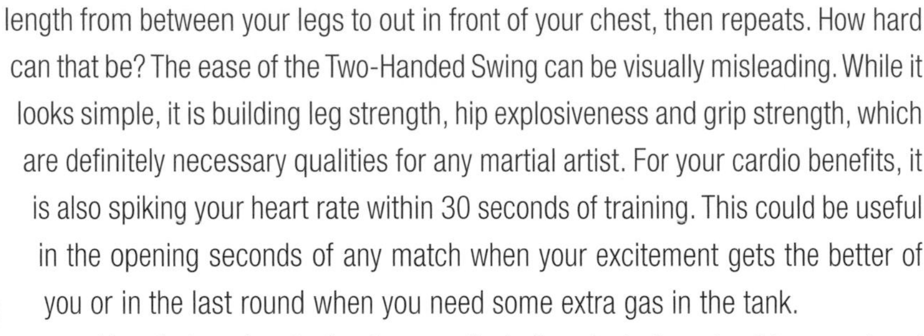

THE TWO-HANDED SWING

Now that you're starting to move the bell explosively and spiking your heart rate, getting tired will be a natural byproduct. With that in mind, now is an excellent time to insist that your kettlebell training take place where you can pitch the bell without worry should something go awry. Never train indoors, such as your living room or on a hard concrete surface. Should you have to abort a rep, and trust me, you will at some point, it's essential to be able to "liberate" your grip with no reservations. Find a suitable outdoor area with plenty of space or an indoor area with mats that won't get damaged should you need to bail.

Also, given the challenging training you will be putting yourself through shortly, remember that proper form of the exercise is paramount. Good form comes from a solid mental understanding of the exercise that is then properly executed by the body. Pay attention to every detail, especially as you begin to tire. You are allowed one bad rep while training. Period. Consistent bad form means higher risk of injury. So if you do more than one bad rep consecutively, *stop* at once to catch your breath and regain your focus. Once you have accomplished this, get back to work. If you can't continue with good form after catching your breath, it's time to call it a day. Never sacrifice form for reps.

Injury is a risk in training and competition. Injuries sustained in competition are hard to control, but during training, you need to minimize that risk as much as possible. Minimizing the risk of injury is accomplished by learning the exercises thoroughly, then focusing your mind on the task at hand and putting out the necessary physical effort. Remember, the body will only perform well if the mind is focused on the physical output.

Increased explosiveness leads to stronger kicks.

Increased grip strength improves weapon retention.

Increased full-body strength is always a benefit.

The Two-Handed Swing

Gentlemen: 16 kg / Ladies: 8 kg

1. Stand behind the bell, approximately six to 12 inches to facilitate the beginning of the Two-Handed Swing.

2. Use the Face-the-Wall-Squat motion to pull yourself back and down to the bell. Let your hands find the handle of the bell, grasp the handle firmly just like you did in the Deadlift. Fire your lats and keep your chest tall.

3. Now use your lats to bring your elbows near your rib cage. Hike the bell behind you like a football—but don't let go! Let the bell move behind you. When your forearms touch your inner thighs, drive your heels into the ground and explosively fire your hips forward so you come up in true Hard-Style-Lock fashion, sending the bell into the air.

(Continued)

The Two-Handed Swing *(Continued)*

4. The bell should begin to arc upward at arm's length. Be sure you are rooted into your heels. Fire your abs and maintain full-body tension while the bell is in the air.

5. At its highest, the apex of the swing is when your arms are parallel to the ground.

Do not lean back to make the bell seem like it's going higher. The height the bell travels is inconsequential compared to the form of the movement you generate to make the bell travel.

6. Don't squat as the bell goes down. Instead, maintain your Hard-Style Lock until your upper arm hits your rib cage. When that happens, that's your cue to release your Hard-Style Lock and squat. This will give you less time to squat, forcing you to squat quicker, so be ready. In maintaining your Hard-Style Lock for as long as possible, you maintain your full-body tension for longer than you would if you squatted as the bell went down. This is good because it builds strength, and strength is a good thing to have.

7. Quickly, pull yourself back and down, such as in the Face-the-Wall Squat, for your next rep.

8. As soon as the bell finishes traveling underneath you, fire your hips again and repeat the movement.

How'd you do? Let's look at some details in the Two-Handed Swing that will help you perform it more properly.

First and foremost, do not lift the bell with your arms. Most people do this because they come to kettlebell training from a bodybuilding type of weightlifting background. That type of lifting does the exact opposite of the kettlebell approach; it isolates muscle groups instead of using the body as a whole to move weight. When doing the Two-Handed Swing, you want to swing the bell with the inertia developed from full-body explosive power. After all, that's why it's called a swing.

More don'ts: Don't lean back to get the bell "higher." Also, don't get pulled onto your toes or lose your balance forward, and don't let your shoulders get pulled forward or let your chest face the floor. Following these rules will help you with additional ballistic exercises down the road.

Do not lift the bell.

Do not lean back.

Do not get pulled onto your toes.

Do not get pulled forward.

Do not round your shoulders; instead, fire your lats.

Do not let your chest face the floor. Keep your chest tall.

You'll know you're doing the Two-Handed Swing properly when the bottom of the bell faces away from you at the top of its arc. This ensures you are not lifting the bell but swinging it as intended. There should be two straight lines when you perform the Two-Handed Swing: One line goes from your heels to your shoulders, and the other from your shoulders to the *bottom* of the bell.

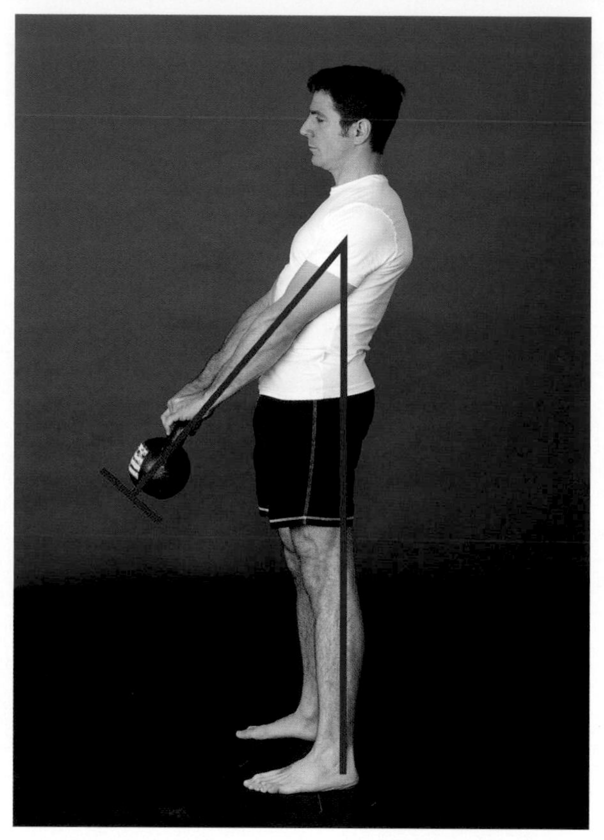

These two straight lines mean you're swinging and not lifting the bell. The height of the swing is inconsequential so long as the lines are straight.

Timing when to squat is often the hardest part of the Two-Handed Swing. It is instinctive to squat while the bell descends in your field of vision, but this will make your swing slow and lethargic, which is the antithesis of hard-style training. Squatting as the kettlebell descends will also bottom out your Two-Handed Swing too low, making your chest face the floor and making you move the kettlebell from a structurally compromised position that unnecessarily puts your lower back at risk. Hold the lock until your forearms are about to hit your hips. Just before they make contact, pull yourself down as quickly and explosively into the squat as you fired them to swing the bell up.

To gauge the proper height of the kettlebell while at the bottom of your ballistic exercises my teacher, Dr. Mark Cheng, uses an analogy of two triangles. The "lower" triangle is made up of three points—your two heels and your groin. The "upper" triangle connects your knees to your groin. Your goal when doing ballistic exercises of any nature is to keep the bell in the upper triangle at the bottom of each rep. This will facilitate a more structurally safe position from which to move weight. The lower you swing the kettlebell, the more likely you are to be pulled onto your toes, which can risk back injury or introduce your face to the floor. Neither of these is optimal for any ballistic exercise. Keeping the kettlebell in the upper triangle is definitely a safer method to swing the bell. Also, this delayed timing on the squat forces you to maintain the Hard-Style Lock longer, which, as you already know, helps you build strength through tension.

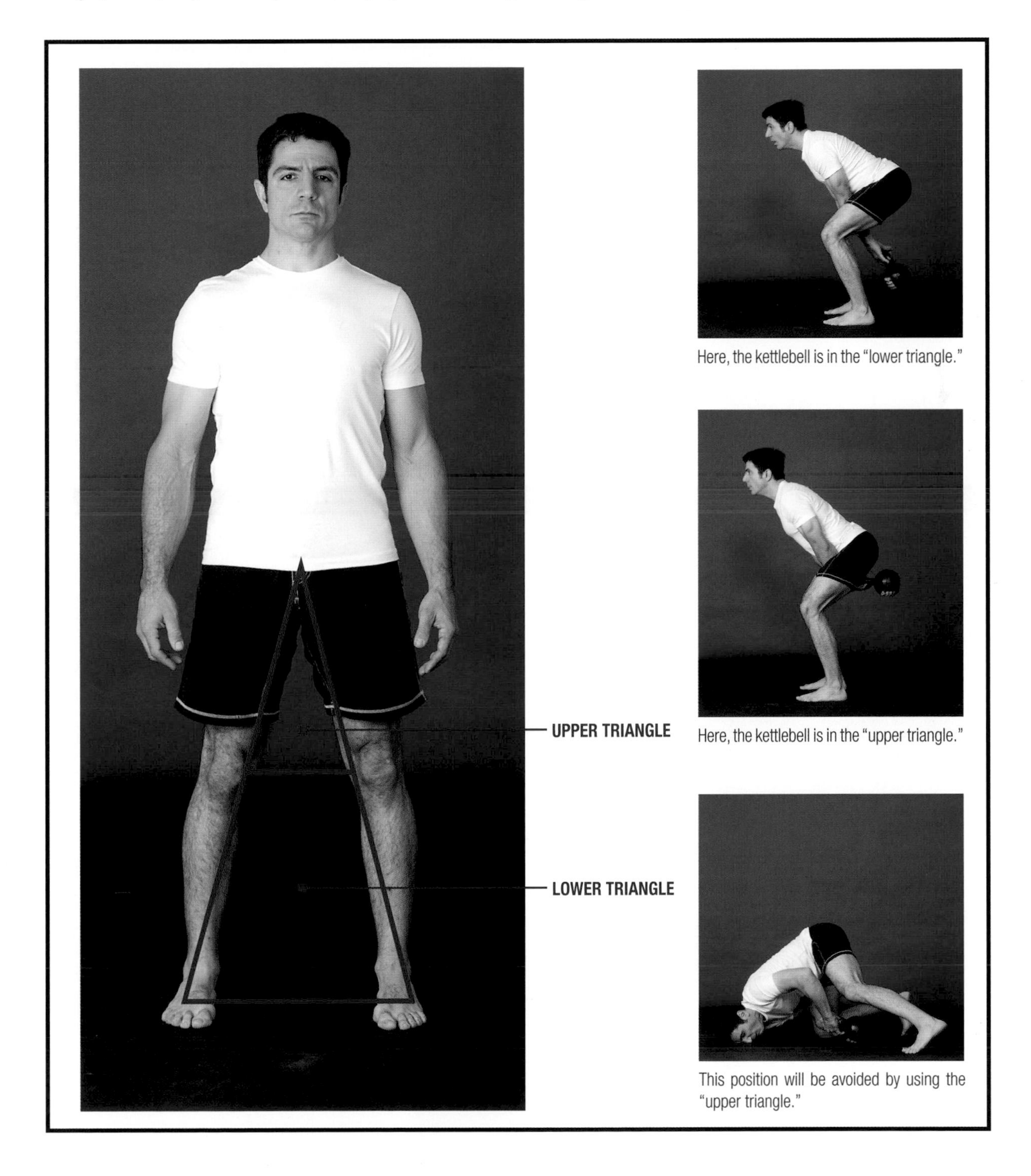

Here, the kettlebell is in the "lower triangle."

Here, the kettlebell is in the "upper triangle."

This position will be avoided by using the "upper triangle."

Soreness or Pain?

What's the difference between soreness and pain? Being sore is the rewarding side effect of hard training. You know you've worked when you experience some soreness afterward. Soreness is OK and even expected. Pain is not. If you experience actual pain when performing any of the exercises in this book, go back to the drawing board and start over because you're doing something wrong. If you are certain you are doing the movements correctly, seek the counsel of a medical professional. Pain is not something to be "pushed through" because you're "tough." Pain is an indicator from your body that you need to stop what you're doing immediately.

After their maiden kettlebell voyage of Two-Handed Swings, most people feel the "feedback" a day or two later in their inner thighs and/or glutes. However, everyone is different, so feel free to start your own trend. Wherever you feel it, the only place you should never feel sore is in your lower back. If you do, it means you are using your arms too much instead of your glutes and legs to move the kettlebell. Although you are starting with a lighter weight, a sore lower back means you need to rely less on your arms and hit your hip snap harder; this minimizes the risk of injury. You might not get hurt on the first day or even the first month, but if you're continually sore in the lower back after hard-style training, you need to realize that it's you and not the exercise. Re-examine the details and start over.

THE TURKISH GET UP

The Turkish Get Up is to grinds what the Two-Handed Swing is to ballistics in that it is the most important. The Turkish Get Up will increase your overall flexibility as well as specific shoulder and hip range of motion. The Turkish Get Up will also increase your strength at odd angles. A wider range of motion that can be moved through with strength is useful in any kind of combat training. The Turkish Get Up will also develop strong, stable wrists that will help you punch better and aid upcoming hard-style exercises such as the Clean, Snatch, Windmill and Military Press.

The Turkish Get Up is a challenging exercise, especially when done with the utmost attention to detail. Many a strong man has been humbled doing this exercise properly with a 16 kg bell. In fact, Dr. Cheng always teaches the "naked" Get Up first, which is how you're going to learn it in this book. Just like with the Face-the-Wall Squat, understand the movements well before putting any weight in your hand. Don't be proud. You could hurt yourself.

OK, here's the training method for the Turkish Get Up, straight from the brain of my coach, Dr. Cheng. To aid the learning process, you will reverse direction every time you do a part of the Turkish Get Up and go back to the beginning. Start over and add the next part to the sequence, then reverse directions

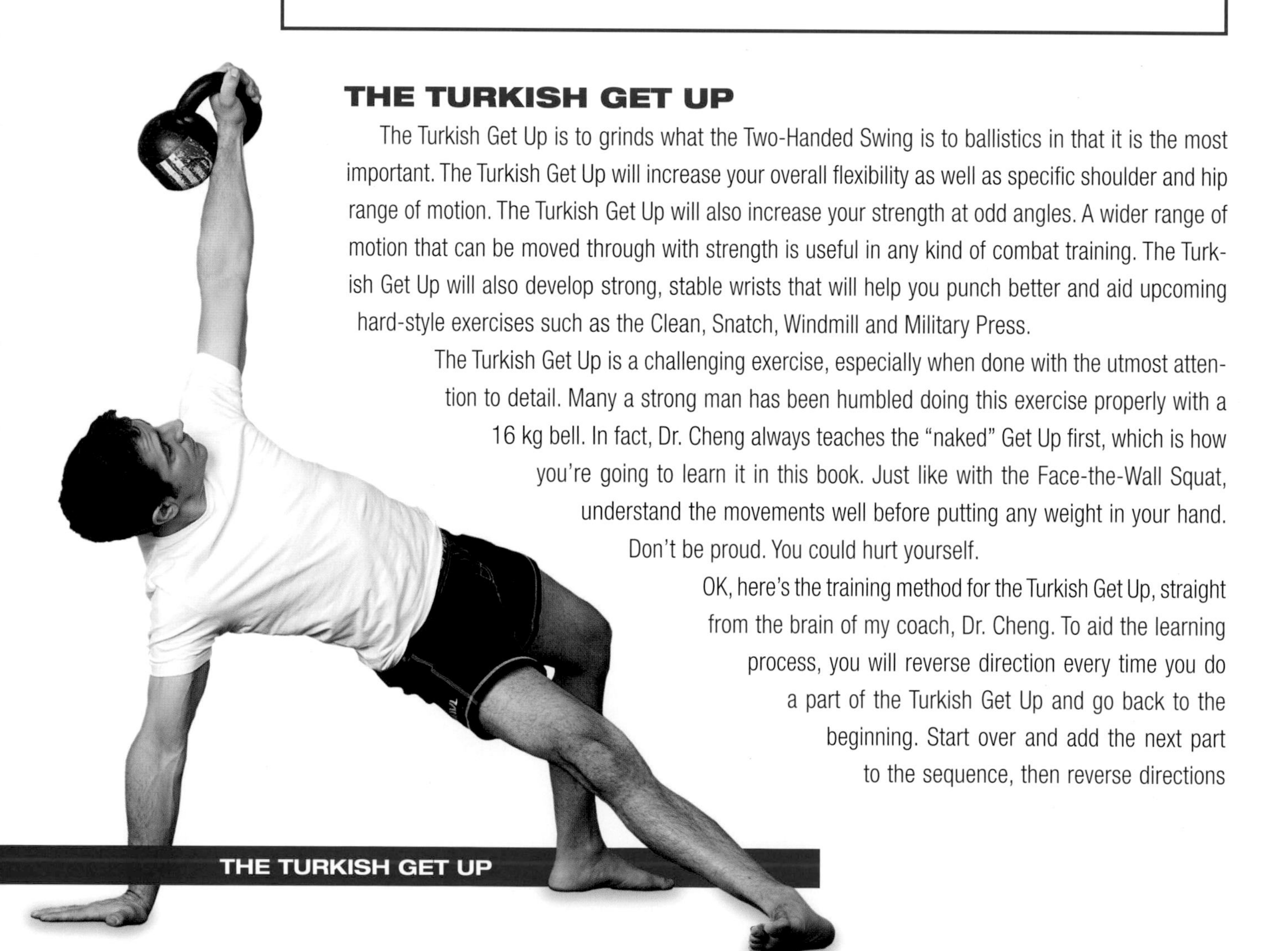
THE TURKISH GET UP

again, etc. You will perform these movements without any weight in hand so you can concentrate on the movements themselves without worrying about stabilizing a cannonball over your noggin.

The Turkish Get Up will increase the range of motion in your shoulder and hip.

Strong wrists from Turkish Get Ups will increase your punching power delivery.

The Turkish Get Up will enhance your balance and movement for fighting from the ground.

Naked Turkish Get Up

Gentlemen: no weight / Ladies: no weight

(Continued)

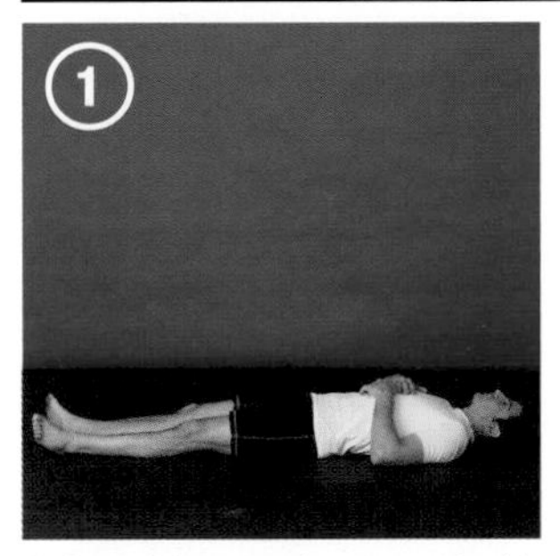
1. Start lying on the ground with the imaginary kettlebell on your right side.

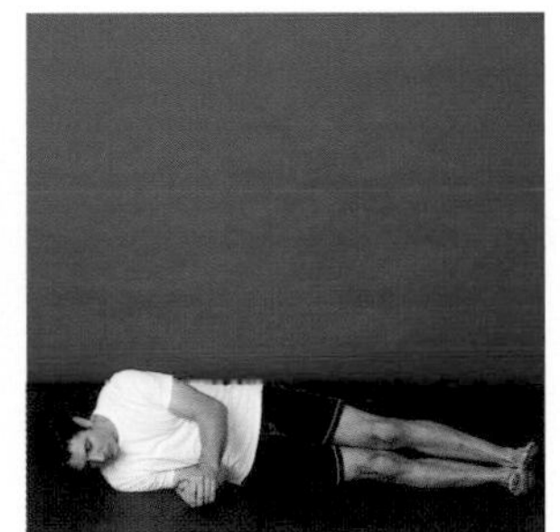
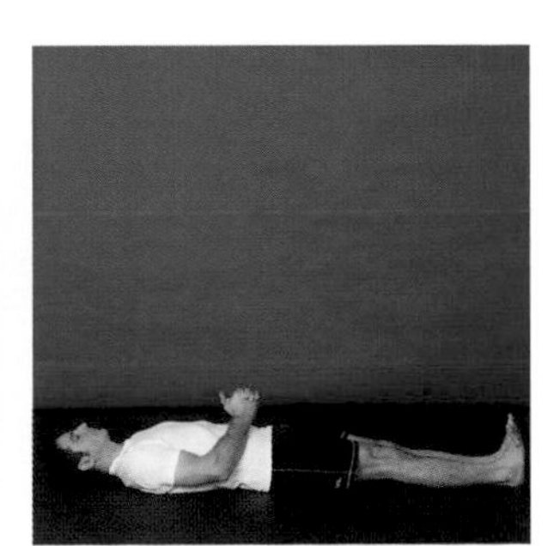

2. Pull and roll: Roll onto your right side, and put your right hand through the handle of the imaginary kettlebell. Cup your left hand over the top of your right hand, and roll onto your back with the imaginary bell resting on your abdomen.
Reverse directions: Roll to your side and dump the imaginary bell. Shake out your hand.

Naked Turkish Get Up *(Continued)*

3. **Firing range:** Pull and roll like you did in Step 2. Keep your grip on the imaginary bell, and straighten your arms to the sky as if you were aiming a handgun. Lock your elbows as straight as they can go. Keep your wrist with the imaginary kettlebell in it straight as if you were delivering a punch. Fire your lats to generate overall core stability, and bring your shoulders into the socket. **Reverse directions:** Pull the bell in with control. Roll to your side and dump the imaginary bell. Shake out your hand.

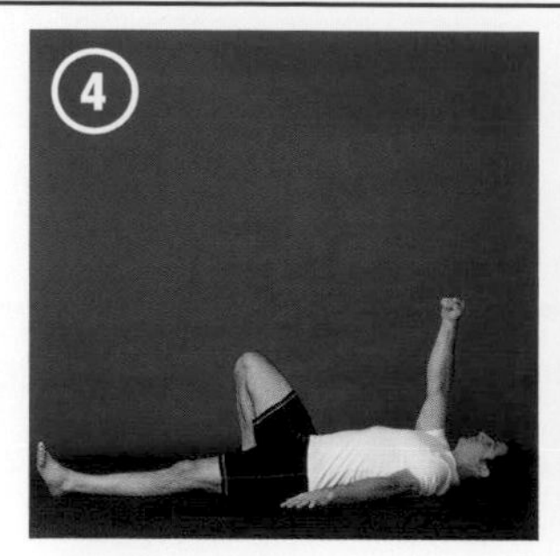

4. **Hand and foot:** Pull and roll, then do the firing range. While keeping your bell-side arm locked straight (in this case the right arm), lower your other arm to the ground and place it at a 45-degree angle from your body. At the same time, bring your bell-side foot close to your butt and a bit wider than your hip. Keep your bell-side elbow locked as straight as possible for the duration of the exercise. This allows your skeleton to support the weight overhead rather than your muscles that will tire quickly. **Reverse directions:** Extend the bell-side leg and return both hands to the firing-range position. Pull the bell in with control. Roll to your side and dump the imaginary bell. Shake out your hand.

5. **Punch and crunch:** Pull and roll, then do the firing-range and hand-and-foot steps. Now combine punching the bell hand upward with doing an active ab crunch. Use the bell-side foot to push you to the opposite side and get your weight up onto the grounded elbow. When you punch, be sure to punch on a diagonal angle that will give you inertia in the direction of your destination: your opposite elbow. Once you get your weight on your unloaded elbow, be sure to push your chest forward and fire both lats to make your torso symmetrical. Pull your shoulders away from your ears and down into the sockets. **Reverse directions:** Return to the hand-and-foot position by slowly lowering yourself onto your back, one vertebra at a time. Return both hands to the firing-range position. Extend the bell-side leg. Pull the bell in, and roll to your side. Dump the imaginary bell, and shake out your hand.

6. **Straighten the arm:** Pull and roll, bring your hands up into the firing-range position, then do the hand and foot and punch and crunch. The kettlebell is now overhead. Your right shoulder is pulled into the socket via the lat engagement. With your weight being supported on your left elbow, straighten your left arm, pivot your left fingers behind you, and roll your shoulder back and down by making sure your support-side lat is firing. Don't let either shoulder shrug toward your ear. **Reverse directions:** Lower your elbow to the ground slowly. Imagine the safe training surface you are on is concrete, so don't slam your elbow into it. Return to hand and foot by slowly lowering yourself onto your back, one vertebra at a time. Return both hands to the firing-range position. Extend the bell-side leg and pull the bell in. Roll to your side, dump the imaginary bell and shake out your hand.

7. **Hips to the sky:** Pull and roll into the firing-range position. Then move into the hand-and-foot, punch-and-crunch and straighten-the-arm positions. With your weight spread evenly between your unloaded hand and both feet, keep the non-bell-side leg straight, and drive your hips to the sky. Make sure you bridge as high as you can, using natural range of motion and any discomfort as your guide. If it hurts, stop. Don't force it. Increases will come gradually.
   Reverse directions: Lower your hips to the ground with control. Lower your elbow to the ground slowly. Return to hand-and-foot position by slowly lowering yourself onto your back, one vertebra at a time. Return both hands to the firing-range position and extend the bell-side leg while pullIng the bell in. Roll to your side, dump the imaginary bell and shake out your hand.

8. **Knee to hand:** Pull and roll into the firing-range position. Then make your way to the hand-and-foot, punch-and-crunch and straighten-the-arm positions. Shoot your hips to the sky. Now you're ready to do the knee to hand. Where the punch-and-crunch step requires some explosive movement, the knee-to-hand step requires a high level of control and coordination to complete without losing your balance. To make this step as controlled as possible, transfer a little more weight to your support hand while still keeping your hips to the sky, thus allowing you to move the extended leg easier. Now bring the knee of that extended leg right next to the supporting hand, preferably touching the wrist. Make sure your bell-side hand remains overhead with a locked elbow and is not tilted forward. When you have a kettlebell in hand, you will understand why.
   Reverse directions: Extend the left leg back out. Raise your hips to the sky, then lower your hips to the ground with control. Lower your elbow to the ground slowly. Return to the hand-and-foot position by slowly lowering yourself onto your back, one vertebra at a time. Return both hands to the firing-range position. Extend the bell-side leg, and pull the bell in. Then roll to your side, dump the imaginary bell and shake out your hand.

9. **Genuflect:** Do the pull-and-roll step to the firing-range position. Then move through the hand-and-foot, punch-and-crunch, straighten-the-arm, hips-to-the-sky and knee-to-hand steps. In order to "genuflect," you need to change your support structure from your hand to your knee. The closer you can get your knee to your wrist in the previous step, the easier this change will be. With your knee touching your wrist, lift your support hand off the ground and pivot your left foot behind you. Tuck your kneeling-side toes underneath. Be certain to keep the bell overhead and retain a locked elbow while still firing the lat through this part of the sequence. I know it's difficult, but do your training and your body a favor: Take the time to really learn how to simultaneously lock the arm out overhead while pulling the shoulder into the socket with the lat.
   Reverse directions: Pivot your left foot underneath you, and close to your right foot. Reach down with your left hand, and transfer your weight from your left knee to your left hand. Extend the left leg back out. Raise your hips to the sky, then lower your hips to the ground with control. Lower your elbow to the ground slowly. Return to the hand-and-foot position by slowly lowering yourself onto your back, one vertebra at a time. Return both hands to the firing-range position, and extend the bell side leg, pulling the bell in. Roll to your side, dump the imaginary bell and shake out your hand.

10. **Stand:** Pull and roll. Make your way to the firing-range position, then move through the hand-and-foot, punch-and-crunch, straighten-the-arm, knee-to-hand and hips-to-sky steps. Genuflect. OK, here's the last part: standing up. Adjust your right foot to an appropriate distance for standing. With one upward and forward step with the left foot, come to the standing position with the imaginary bell in the overhead, locked-out position.
    Reverse directions: Take a deep enough step backward with your non-bell-side foot to facilitate *slowly* lowering your left knee to the ground. Too narrow a stance will make it difficult to lower your knee. Your knee should not make a sound when it makes contact with the ground; your touchdown is soft. Pivot your left foot underneath you, and reach down with your left hand to transfer your weight from your left knee to your left hand. Extend the left leg back out. Raise your hips to the sky, then lower your hips to the ground with control. Lower your elbow to the ground slowly. Return to the hand-and-foot position by slowly lowering yourself onto your back, one vertebra at a time. Return both hands to the firing-range position, and extend the bell-side leg. Pull the bell in, roll to your side, dump the imaginary bell and shake out your hand.

This step-by-step method is done to accelerate the learning process. Once you have done the exercise a few times in this manner, just go through it in sequence from beginning to end without reversing the motions.

The Turkish Get Up is arguably the most important exercise in the entire hard-style system, so let's review some of the key points. Remember to keep the loaded-side elbow fully locked from the firing-range position until you finish the sequence. Also, be sure to fire your lats through the entire exercise to keep your shoulders in a safe position. Additionally, make sure the loaded wrist is straight. Finally, move deliberately and with control. A good pace for a Turkish Get Up is about one minute per rep. If you're doing it faster than that (even without a bell), you're doing it too fast. Take your time to move up in weight. Don't go too big, too fast. Learn the movement well with a 16 or 8 kg bell. In the beginning, when you're practicing with lighter bells and you're starting to get coordinated with the movement, force yourself to separate the steps with distinct pauses. There is no need to do a Turkish Get Up with a 32 kg bell or bigger during your first month on the exercise if ever. It's far more important to move whatever bell you use with stability and execute the movement pattern down to the finest details. Remember the kettlebell is the tool and not the goal. Do it right.

Variations on the Turkish Get Up

For reasons of safety alone, I have explained the Turkish Get Up in body-weight format only. If you can complete a Naked Turkish Get Up with all the attention to detail that I have outlined for the exercise, try these additional versions:

1. **Double-Up Naked Turkish Get Up:** For the Double-Up Naked Turkish Get Up, simply perform every part of the standard issue naked version as already outlined twice before moving on to the next part. For example, pull and roll twice before moving to the firing range. Then do the firing range twice before doing the hand and foot twice, etc. If you want to reverse the motions, go ahead, but it's not required. Either way, make certain that every stop along the way, you execute the details. Keep the lats firing, and make sure your knee is in good position. Push your chest forward and dial in with proper lat tension, knee position, chest pushed open, etc. Everything is the same as a standard-issue Naked Turkish Get Up, but you're just repeating the movements twice before adding on the next one.
2. **Triple-Up Naked Turkish Get Up:** This is the same idea as the Double-Up version, but now do the individual parts three times before moving on. This might not sound too challenging, but if you truly focus on the details, you will feel how demanding it is.
3. **Turkish Get Up With Weight:** Once you can perform the Turkish Get Up well in the above methods, then you can try it with a kettlebell. I would prefer you only attempt a loaded Turkish Get Up with a training partner spotting you throughout the entire sequence. With just about any other hard-style exercise, you can abort at will. If/when you lose control while you're in one of the more precarious sections of the Turkish Get Up, you're either going to be singing falsetto or visiting the dentist. Have a training partner spot you through the exercise should something go wrong. Safety first folks!

Using a Spotter

Given the complexity of the Turkish Get Up and the precarious positions you are in throughout the sequence, there is one special safety note. Once you are intimately familiar with the Naked Turkish Get Up exercise and confident in your ability to attempt it loaded, be sure to have a training partner around to spot you on your first weighted attempts. Make sure whoever is spotting you has their hands in position below the bell for the duration of the exercise. If/when the Turkish Get Up goes "south," it will get ugly fast, so your partner needs to be ready to immediately stabilize the bell or pull it away from you the instant it becomes necessary.

Be certain your spotter stays close but does not impede your movement through the exercise. His hands should be *physically* under the kettlebell for the duration of your Turkish Get Up. This will allow him to help you immediately should you need assistance.

The Turkish Get Up

Gentlemen: 16 kg / Ladies: 8 kg

(Continued)

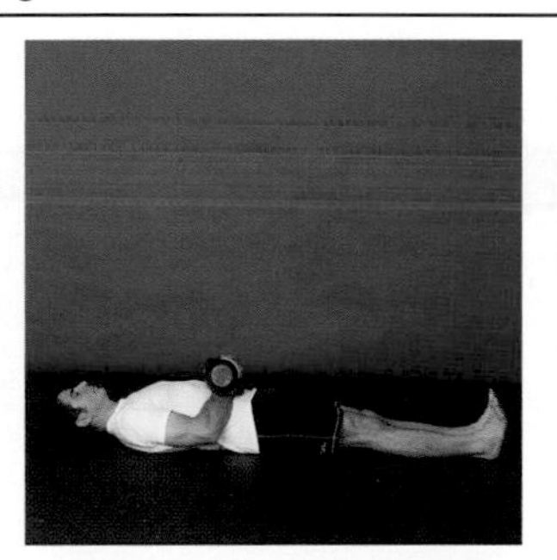

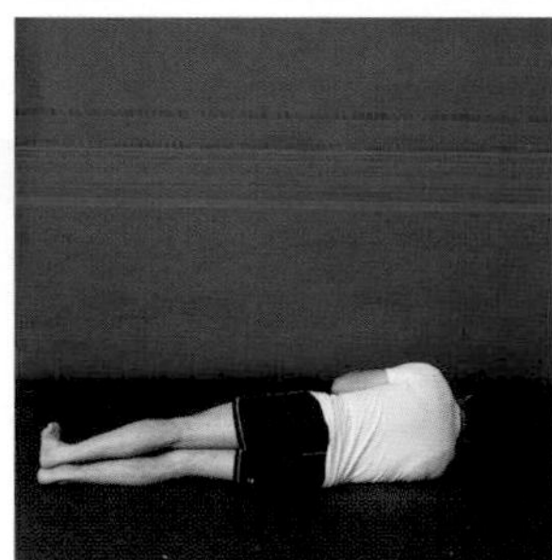

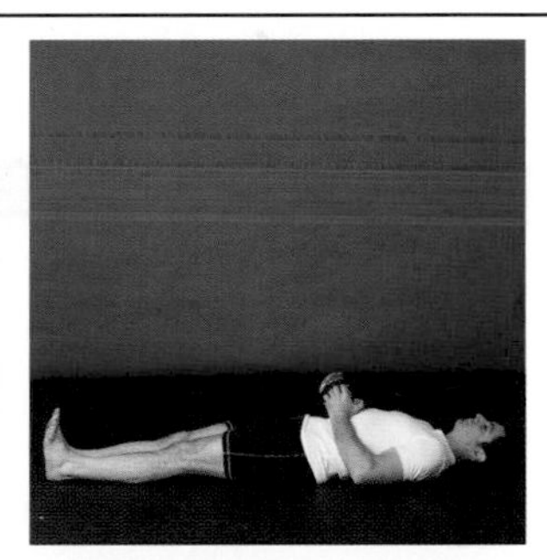

1. **Pull and roll:** Roll onto your right side, and put your right hand through the handle of the kettlebell. Cup your left hand over the top of your right hand. Roll onto your back with the bell resting on your abdomen.

2. **Firing range:** Now keeping your grip on the bell, straighten your arms to the sky as if you were firing a handgun. Lock your elbows as straight as they can go, and keep your loaded wrist straight as if you were delivering a punch. Fire your lats to bring your shoulders into the socket.

3. **Hand and foot:** Pull and roll, then move into the firing-range position. While keeping your bell-side arm locked straight, lower your other arm to the ground and place it at a downward 45-degree angle from your shoulder. At the same time, bring your bell-side foot close to your butt and a bit wider than your hip. Rather than pulling the heel close, place the ball of the foot as close to your butt as possible, then lower the heel; it will be closer than before. Keep your bell-side elbow locked and as straight as possible for the duration of the exercise. Do not unlock your elbow!

The Turkish Get Up *(Continued)*

4. **Punch and crunch:** Depending on the size bell, this is the one part of the sequence that needs to be done with some intention. Using a combination of punching upward with the bell hand, doing an ab crunch and using the bell-side foot to push yourself to the opposite side, get your weight up onto the elbow that is on the grounded arm. A few things people do that makes this part difficult is they try to punch straight up into the sky. They usually end up doing an ugly partial crunch, and the extended leg rises up into the air. When you punch, be sure to punch on a diagonal angle that will give you inertia in the direction of your destination: your opposite elbow. Also, the reason you place your bell-side foot wider than the hip is so you can use the foot to help get up onto your elbow. Once you reach the point at which you are balanced on your opposite elbow, be sure to push your chest forward and fire both lats to pull your elbows away from your ears. This will keep your torso symmetrical as well as your shoulders stable and safe.

5. **Straighten the arm:** With your weight being supported on your left elbow, straighten the arm and pivot your left fingers behind you. Be sure to keep the lat fired once the arm is straightened; don't let your shoulder shrug toward your ear.

6. **Hips to the sky:** Keep the non-bell-side leg straight and drive your hips to the sky. Make sure you really bridge as high as you can. Get as much range of motion out of your hips as you can while simultaneously requiring stability from both shoulders.

7. **Knee to hand:** Whereas the punch-and-crunch step requires some explosive movement, knee to hand demands the most coordination. Getting your knee to your hand is very important and difficult for first-timers. I see a lot of people get their knee under their body, then have to scramble their way to the next movement. Still others pull their leg straight underneath them and run out of room before their knee is in proper position. There is no reason to put your body in such jeopardy, so let's master this challenging step. While in the hips-to-the-sky position, transfer a little more weight to your support hand and your bell-side foot, thus allowing you to move the extended leg easier. Now bend that extended leg at the knee, and bring the extended foot in a circle right next to your bell-side foot. Once the swiveling foot has passed the bell-side foot, move the knee of your swiveling leg right next to the supporting hand, preferably touching the wrist. The closer you can get this knee to this hand, the better, which will be evident in the next part of the sequence. Make sure your bell-side hand remains overhead with a locked elbow and is not tilted forward. With a bell in that hand, it will be imperative to remain vertical with a locked elbow.

8. Genuflect: At this point, you'll transfer your support structure from your hand to your knee. The closer your knee can be to your wrist (preferably touching), the easier this transfer will be. The farther the distance between hand and knee, the more dangerous this moment becomes. With your knee touching your wrist, lift your support hand off the ground and pivot your left foot behind you. Tuck your kneeling-side toes underneath. The difficulty everyone has at this point is keeping the bell overhead and retaining a locked elbow while still firing the lat to maintain the shoulder in a safe position. What most people do is lock the elbow and shrug the shoulder to the ear or they pull the shoulder down and unlock the elbow. Neither of these is acceptable. Shrugging puts your collarbone, neck and shoulder at risk. Releasing the elbow lock requires your muscles to do what your skeletal system should be doing. I know it's difficult, but take the time to really learn how to simultaneously lock the arm out overhead while pulling the shoulder into the socket with the lat.

9. Stand: OK, here's the last part. Adjust your right foot to an appropriate distance for standing, and with one upward and forward step with the left foot, come to a standing position with the bell in the overhead, locked-out position.

Motivation: Finding and Maintaining It

If you remember one thing from this book, remember there are no overnight successes. You need to put in the time before you reap the rewards. Dr. Muang Gyi, grandmaster of *bando*, has two simple rules for martial arts training, which are equally appropriate for hard-style kettlebell training. The first rule is don't be lazy. The second rule is never be too proud to learn. If you apply Dr. Gyi's rules to both areas of your training (and to your life in general), you will surprise yourself with your successes.

I knew a woman years ago who was a successful fitness and diet personality. One of her sayings was, "Stop waiting for the motivating." I meet people all the time who want to train martial arts or kettlebells but think like they have to get in shape before they start training. Call me crazy, but isn't that one of the primary points of training? Why get fit *before* you start? With that mind-set, you will never start. People frequently talk themselves out of doing something before they even begin. If you never start working, you'll never get paid. So get to work, and you will get the results you seek. Motivation arrives shortly after the work begins. Once you start getting the results, don't sit back and chill. Maintain your motivation and keep pushing forward because there is a lot to learn. Don't do it halfway.

Your Expectations

Once you learn these new exercises, you'll be wondering when you can expect results. In my experience, many people who begin using hard-style kettlebells see changes within a few training sessions. This is not surprising because kettlebell exercises will be a shock to your body, and it will respond.

As Marty Gallagher says in his brilliant book, *The Purposeful Primitive*, the body is "subject to biological imperatives." If you impose a "specific resistance protocol of sufficient intensity" on your body, you will get stronger. That's great, but what happens in a few months when the movement is no longer a shock to the body? Human nature strives for efficiency in physical activity, meaning you will eventually reach a point of diminishing returns if you maintain the same training regimen. Your results will stagnate. The upcoming variety of exercises is not just to keep those of you with short attention spans interested. It's also meant to keep your body surprised by what you impose on it. If you keep that element of surprise prevalent in your training, improvements will continue. Perform these exercises with high intensity, total commitment and strict observation to the details, and you will get the strength, conditioning and flexibility gains you are looking for.

THE GOBLET SQUAT

The Goblet Squat is the preferred method to introduce hard-style kettlebell practitioners to squatting exercises. It trains the movement pattern and increases leg strength and hip flexibility while also developing upper-body stability. Hip and groin flexibility are fundamental attributes of any combative endeavor. If your goal is to someday kick your opponent above the ankle, improve regaining/retaining your guard while on your back, or expand your repertoire of footwork while on your feet, then strengthening your legs and increasing your hip flexibility had better be a priority.

Although there are many choices of squats in the hard-style curriculum, the Goblet Squat is the first one taught because of its simplicity and inherently safe design. The kettlebell is held in front of and close to the chest during the exercise. The upper-body stability and more vertical spine required to support the weight in this position place the load on the legs and glutes where it belongs, not the back. Also, if necessary, the exercise can be aborted safely by just lowering the bell to the ground.

Similar to a Deadlift, you always want to use major muscle groups like your quads and glutes to do the work when you squat. It is important to note that although the Deadlift and loaded Goblet Squat movements are similar, the hard-style party line notes slight distinctions between the two. When performing a Deadlift, the pelvis moves back and down. On a Goblet Squat, the pelvis moves down and only slightly back. If you're new, don't over-think it just yet. Give yourself a few thousand reps before you start expending brain power on the differences. For now, just remember that the Face-the-Wall Squat teaches proper form for ballistic exercises and the Goblet Squat teaches the fundamentals of squatting exercises.

THE GOBLET SQUAT

The Goblet Squat

Gentlemen: 16 kg / Ladies: 8 kg

1. Standing with your feet strictly parallel and shoulder-width apart, grasp the bell by the "horns." With a slight swinging motion, hoist the bell upward. Keep your grip on the "horns," and hold the bell close to your chest. Squeeze the body of the bell with your forearms.

2. Similar to the Face-the-Wall Squat, pull yourself down between your feet as far as you can with good form.

3. Come back up to a standing position-with a solid HSL.

4. Repeat the Goblet Squat with the same attention to detail, but this time, pull yourself a little lower into the squat.

5. Come back up to a standing position in a solid HSL.

6. Continue this "getting deeper" sequence until the fifth rep, at which point you should "bottom out," meaning you go as low as you possibly can while maintaining good form. If you can't actually put your butt on your heels, that's OK. Just go as far as you can with good form and let your forearms slide inside your legs. Again, like in the TGU, let your natural range of motion and any discomfort be your guide.

7. Stay at the bottom, keep your chest tall and gently rock your weight from side to side, opening your hips and groin up a little more each time. Do this for at least 10 seconds.

8. After rocking back and forth, let the bell down to the ground and come up with good form. Hit a naked HSL at the top.

This exercise is intended to teach good squat form, so don't do it wrong. Work hard to keep your feet as close to parallel throughout your entire squat. If the toes point out, make sure the knees track over them.

Bad Squatting Posture

This is bad knee position relative to the toes.

Good Squatting Posture

Keep the knees tracking over the toes. If necessary, use your elbows to help push your knees out.

THE ONE-HANDED SWING

The One-Handed Swing is half of the 2HSW but twice the work. While the 2HSW is the foundational ballistic exercise of the system, it is an exercise that requires two hands to complete. With two hands on the kettlebell, the load on each shoulder is equal, making the 2HSW symmetrical by its very nature. With only one hand on the bell, the One-Handed Swing is asymmetrical by nature and it requires double the grip strength and double the upper-body stability at the top of the arc and the bottom.

Improved grip strength from one-handed work has obvious combative advantages for weaponry practitioners. Ground grapplers and standing-clinch specialists will also experience improved asymmetrical stability. In addition, the One-Handed Swing is also the necessary first step in getting you into the neighborhood of other single-handed ballistics exercises such as the Clean and the Snatch. All single-handed exercises will help bring power finesse, which is the ability to be smooth with your power delivery, and high-volume endurance work to your training.

As mentioned, the One-Handed Swing differs from the 2HSW in only one way: how many hands are on the bell. Everything

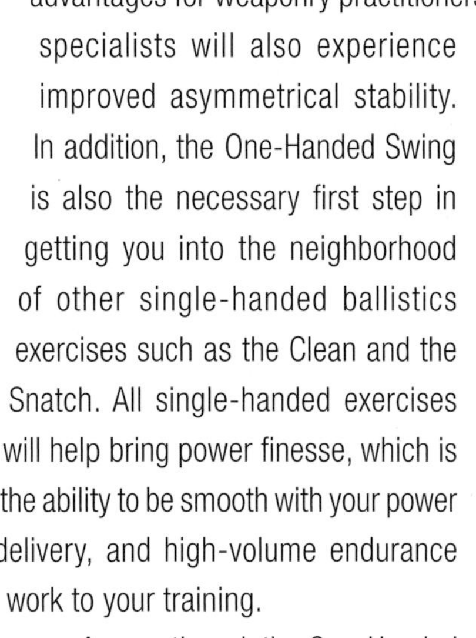

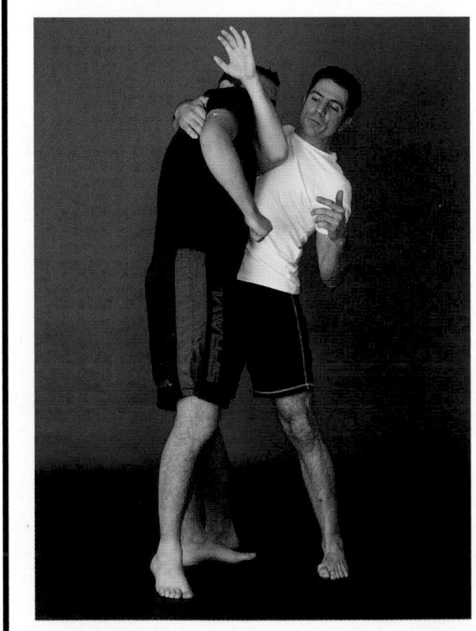

The One-Handed Swing will increase your asymmetrical strength.

else is literally the same, but like most hard-style things, this is easier said than done. With only one hand on the bell, you will feel a tug trying to pull your loaded side forward at the top and bottom of the swing's arc, the intensity of which is determined by the size bell being swung. The stability required to counteract that forward pull cannot be disregarded. You need to generate more tension on the loaded side in order to stay square and balanced throughout the exercise, which is the goal. Use your bell-side lat to keep the loaded shoulder pulled back and down into the socket and your chest square to the bell throughout the entire movement. This is difficult at first, so be patient and diligent. This is also why you're using a 16/8 kg bell at first because it will challenge but not injure you. When you finish a set on the left, stop. Put the kettlebell down, switch hands and do an equal number of reps on the right so the body remains balanced.

The One-Handed Swing

Gentlemen: 16 kg / Ladies: 8 kg

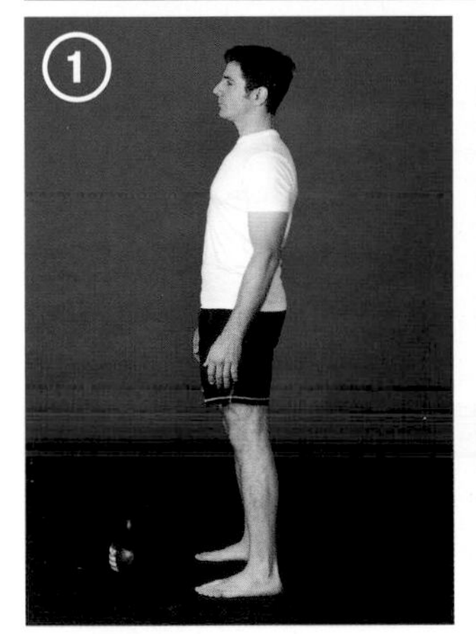

1. Stand behind the bell like you would for a 2HSW.

2. Pull yourself back and down in the same squat pattern as the 2HSW, but this time, grasp the handle with only one hand. You can use your empty hand out to the side for counterbalance, but do not let it cheat by pushing on your thigh to take some of the weight off your lower body.

3. Keeping your chest square, hike the bell between your legs.

4. When your forearm hits your inner thigh, fire your hips and glutes in explosive Hard-Style-Lock fashion to send the bell on its course.

5. The kettlebell will follow the same arm's length arc it took during the 2HSW. Keep your chest square. Do not get pulled forward on the bell side at the top of the arc.

6. Maintain your HSL while the bell descends.

7. Release the HSL as your upper arm is about to touch your rib cage.

8. Pull yourself quickly into the squat and fire another swing. Repeat for 10 reps, then switch hands by placing the bell on the ground.

Bad Swing Form

The loaded side will want to go forward at the top.

The loaded side will want to go lower at the bottom.

Good Swing Form

Maintain a square chest at the top.

Do not let the loaded side get pulled out of square.

THE SWING SWITCH

THE SWING SWITCH

Cardiovascular conditioning is something all martial artists need regardless of discipline. If you're not in shape for a competition or to defend yourself on the street, you're in trouble. The quickest method to increase your cardio capacity is to extend your training time. As your form improves, you will find that you can train for a longer duration. Whereas the first time you tried the 2HSW, you lasted 30 seconds, now you can go for 45 seconds. This is good!

When performing single-handed ballistic exercises on one side of the body, switching hands is essential to maintaining balance between the right and left sides. To switch sides with the One-Handed Swing, I had you stop, place the bell on the ground and change hands to balance out your training. When new to one-handed ballistics, this is the best method to switch hands without risking injury; the downside is that switching hands breaks up your training momentum. To continue the intensity of your training without breaking your stride, you will want to switch hands without having to stop. This task is accomplished with the Swing Switch. The Swing Switch is a One-Handed Swing that starts in one hand, reaches its apex and switches to the other hand while momentarily weightless.

Change hands while in motion? Isn't that dangerous? What happened to all that talk about safety? Well, it requires some practice, but if done at the right time, it's not dangerous. If the timing of when you release your grip on the bell is correct, you can let go at the top of any Swing when the bell is momentarily weightless before it begins its descent back to earth. (This is the essence of catch-and-release training, which you'll hit more in depth later in the book.) The Swing Switch is timed for this weightless moment. If you let go too early, the bell will fly away from you. If you let go too late, you won't have as much time to see it float. With these two concerns in mind, only try the Swing Switch in a place where you won't worry about the bell taking a header if your timing is off.

The Swing Switch
Gentlemen: 16 kg / Ladies: 8 kg

1. Perform five One-Handed Swings to get a sense of the timing for when the bell is "weightless."

2. As the bell reaches the apex of its arc on the fifth rep, have your empty hand waiting to receive the bell.

3. Let the back of your gripping hand hit the palm of your empty hand. You're using it as a guide to make a quick switch. Release the bell from your grip, and re-grip the bell with your other hand. You have successfully switched sides without stopping the exercise. Perform five One-Handed Swings to balance out your training and switch back to the original hand on the fifth rep.

There will be any number of occasions when your timing is off, and in any and all those cases, *do not* reach for the bell to try to catch it. That's why you train where you have no worries about the kettlebell meeting the ground with force. Damaging the kettlebell and/or the training floor are not your primary concerns. Safety dictates that if you lose control of the bell, you just let it fly. Allow gravity to take the bell to the ground, then pick it up and get back to training.

THE CLEAN

The Clean is our second single-handed ballistic exercise. It follows the same lower-body squatting movement of the 2HSW and One-Handed Swing but also teaches new skills that will pay dividends with future exercises and your combat skills. The Clean is a multilayered exercise that regulates your power output to be task appropriate, keeps your wrist in good punching alignment, reinforces good elbow position for strong defense, and pressurizes your abdomen to both replicate a virtual shield against incoming firepower and help move the kettlebell overhead for future exercises such as the Military Press. Sounds like a lot, right? It is.

Similar to strength training with the Olympic bar, the kettlebell has many lifts that move the weight overhead and finish with a straight elbow. This is known as the overhead lockout. The Olympic-bar exercises include the Clean and Jerk and the Military Press, to name a couple without going into too much detail. The Military Press moves the bar from shoulder height, also known as the rack, to the overhead lockout with no inertia. This is similar to how the Deadlift from the last chapter is not executed with explosiveness but with raw strength. On the other hand, with the Clean and Jerk, the lifter first moves a weight explosively from the ground to the rack position. This movement is known on its own as a Power Clean. Then with the aid of a simultaneous squat in the legs, the lifter "jerks" the weight upward while ducking underneath the bar and straightening his arms, at which point he stands upright with the bar overhead and his arms locked out.

Because the goal when doing strength training for the sake of strength training is to move as much weight as possible, the Clean portion of the Clean and Jerk really just facilitates jerking bigger weight overhead. For this reason, many kettlebellers who come from a "strength only" perspective see the Clean with the kettlebell merely as a means to get a larger bell overhead via a Jerk or a Push Press, which both use the legs to initiate the bell's upward movement. This book, however, is about using kettlebells to complement your martial arts training. A good Clean for the martial artist who trains kettlebells moves the bell silently and gently to the rack. From here, the bell can be moved overhead by any of the means already listed, or you can retain the bell in the rack to reinforce strong defensive posture and good wrist position for punching. For these reasons, I highly recommend you not underestimate the Clean and its requisite fine touch or be scared off by its difficulty as a novice. It has a lot to offer.

THE CLEAN

Where the 2HSW requires full power every time, the Clean is a technique that requires "task appropriate" force. This means you only generate exactly the amount of force needed to accomplish the task. No more, no less. The Clean is a "finesse" exercise that requires simultaneous fluidity of motion and physical control to land the kettlebell softly and silently in the rack. Finesse in martial arts is underemphasized in training and underused in competition. How many times have you sparred in class and it's just become a wild slugfest? Or you go to a Brazilian jiu-jitsu competition in which your regularly "crafty" self is replaced by a bull in a china shop none of your teammates recognize. Using maximum power can easily make you overcommit to your attack and leave you open to counterstrikes and, often worse, premature exhaustion. Moving with finesse makes what you do look effortless and verifies that your physical output is appropriate for the task at hand with a strong focus on timing and accuracy.

A kettlebell Clean done with the full-force hip snap of a 2HSW will beat up your forearm inside of a dozen reps. Remember the soft and silent landing from above? This landing is essential for acceptable execution of a Clean. A soft landing means you have tempered your power output appropriate for the task. Try the following experiment: Have your training partner hold a focus mitt for you to punch and have him tell you what degree of force with which to hit the mitt. He should mix up the percentages at random—30 percent, 70 percent, 100 percent, etc. You do single punches of whatever he calls out. Do this for 10 reps, being certain to have him call out a different intensity each time so you can accurately gauge your power output. Now perform 10 rapid-fire punches at 80 percent. Take a breather. Once you catch your breath, perform 10 more rapid-fire punches, this time at 100 percent. Go ahead, do it now. Done? OK, how much difference did your partner holding the focus mitt notice between the 80-percent and 100-percent punches? If you were accurate in your force delivery, he probably didn't feel much difference at all. But you felt a huge difference didn't you? You felt a lot more winded. Your heart rate increased a lot, and you might even have broken a little sweat from just those few full-intensity punches. In short, the effort-to-result ratio hits a wall here. Your partner feels nearly the same power at 80 percent as he does at 100 percent, but you feel like you've done twice as much work, and for zero-added effectiveness! So, in essence, while a Clean mimics the squat pattern of the 2HSW, it does not have the full-intensity hip snap of the Swing. The Clean maintains the crispness but adjusts the intensity of your hip snap, depending on the size bell you're using.

The second crucial difference between the Swing and the Clean is the movement of the elbow, or lack thereof. After executing a kettlebell Clean, the elbow is glued to the torso directly beneath the load. Positioning the elbow close to the torso is important in a variety of sensitivity-based arts and sports in which the elbow is a key to upper-body control—wrestling, *wing chun*, *jeet kune do*, muay Thai clinch, Brazilian jiu-jitsu, etc. If I can get past your elbow, you're in trouble in those martial arts and vice versa. With the elbow near the rib cage, the lat is at its strongest and will assist your mount escape, make it harder for someone to arm-drag you or land effective shots to your flank. Elbow position is equally significant in weaponry. *Balintawak* grandmaster Nene Gaabucayan emphasizes the importance of this tight elbow position when he teaches stick fighting. He keeps the elbow "clipped" to the hip, limiting the arm's tendency to reach, which leaves you open to countless attacks.

Proper wrist alignment is necessary for effective punching.

The limited elbow movement of the Clean facilitates bringing the kettlebell up on a nearly vertical path. Whereas the 2HSW has an arm's length arc, the Clean uses little to no arc at all. When performing a Clean, you should think about "zipping up your jacket" as soon as the kettlebell clears your legs and groin. The lack of a "tamed" arc when performing the Clean is the reason most people beat up their forearm when learning the exercise. A One-Handed Swing that ends up in the rack is not a Clean, and you will be sore. Be certain to tame the arc of the Clean to get the soft and silent landing you want.

Greasing the Groove

There will always be problematic movement patterns for everyone. You might have tremendous success early in your training, but stumbling blocks will eventually arise at some point. The Clean is often a training hiccup for many people. One of the best ways to get lots of reps in without gassing yourself is to "grease the groove." Simply put, greasing the groove means you do freakishly low numbers of reps (one to five) of a movement or exercise throughout the course of the day. If you work at a desk, leave your bell nearby, and every time you get up and sit down, perform three reps of whatever exercise is bugging you. (You won't run the risk of grip fatigue because of the low reps, but make sure you have enough space for the exercise so you don't inadvertently trash the office.)

Those few reps at regular intervals throughout the course of the day will easily and quickly add up. Even just going to the restroom, you will probably do at least a few dozen reps per day, and that's not counting all the other times you stand up and sit down. It's not difficult to get 100-plus reps in of any exercise with this protocol.

Do these reps to really focus on the specific details of the movement in order to dial in your performance. The Clean was a challenging exercise for me at first. My forearms were constantly sore. Greasing the groove was the only way I got a handle on the exercise without beating myself up too badly in training.

The rack directly relates to a good defensive position.

The straight-wrist position of the Clean reinforces good punching form. It also minimizes the tendinitis and grip fatigue brought on by pointing your palm upward in the rack or overhead lockout during high-rep ballistic training. Once cleaned to the rack, the kettlebell rests in the "V" made by your forearm and upper arm. The wrist is locked straight, do not let your palm face upward. Also, if a press of some kind is your goal after cleaning the bell to the rack, the abdominal pressurization from a solid HSL will assist in moving the kettlebell overhead. In short, do not relax after the bell lands in the rack position. As you can see, the Clean is a challenging exercise but with the proper focus on the details, not insurmountable.

The racked bell rests in the "V" of your arm.

Do not let your wrist bend to the weight.

The Clean

Gentlemen: 16 kg / Ladies: 8 kg

1. Stand behind the kettlebell as if you are setting up for a One-Handed Swing. Grab the bell like you did for the One-Handed Swing.

2. Keeping one hand off your thigh, grasp the handle with the other hand and move the bell beneath and behind you, getting a good back swing.

3. Move the bell forward by firing your hips and hitting your HSL. "Zip up your jacket" as the bell clears your groin. Make the bell travel as vertically as possible toward the rack.

4. Holding your HSL, the bell should come to rest gently in the "V" that is made by your forearm and your upper arm when in the rack position.

5. Lower the bell by straightening your arm down to the ground. Similar to the 2HSW, let gravity bring the bell down, but maintain your HSL for as long as possible.

6. Pull yourself explosively back and down like you did for the One-Handed Swing. Allow the bell to move behind you and fire again. Perform 10 reps. Perform a Swing Switch, then do 10 reps on the opposite side.

THE MILITARY PRESS

The Military Press is one of my favorite exercises. Grinding out a strict Military Press trips a primal trigger like few exercises do for me. Perhaps it harkens back to caveman days, I don't know, but it's just raw and fun.

Proper execution of the Military Press requires full-body tension, generates shoulder mobility and stability, and establishes a stable wrist and crushing grip. Like all grinds, the Military Press demands exceptional stability and major muscle recruitment at the same time. Because the bell ends in the overhead lockout, the shoulder and lats are targeted for the job. You'll also have the added bonus of gaining familiarization with the overhead lockout for the Snatch, which is coming soon.

The Military Press will increase your shoulder strength and mobility.

Straight wrists are good for punching and pressing.

Crushing the handle of the bell while pressing will give you a strong grip for improved weapon retention.

THE MILITARY PRESS

Irradiation

Tension equals strength, and in order to generate the strength needed to do the Military Press well, you will use a concept known as "irradiation." In Step 1 of the Military Press, be certain to "white-knuckle" your empty hand. Why? The tension generated through recruiting the muscles on the unloaded side builds stability in your body and actually makes the Military Press easier to accomplish. You're still moving the same weight; you're just generating more tension, which means more strength, and focusing your mind more on the task.

Take a moment to make yourself a believer with this experiment: Make your way through the Military Press. Go through all the movements as described, but skip the part about white-knuckling your other arm. Relax your non-bell-side hand and arm to see what the Military Press feels like without it. Now repeat the sequence, but this time with irradiation on your side. You will believe.

The Military Press

Gentlemen: 16 kg / Ladies: 8 kg

1. Clean the bell to the rack position. Crush the handle with everything you've got and clench your other fist so it white-knuckles.

2. Start the Press by peeling your loaded elbow away from your torso. Start straightening it upward while maintaining the bell vertically above your elbow.

3. Continue pressing the bell upward while maintaining your elbow position below the load.

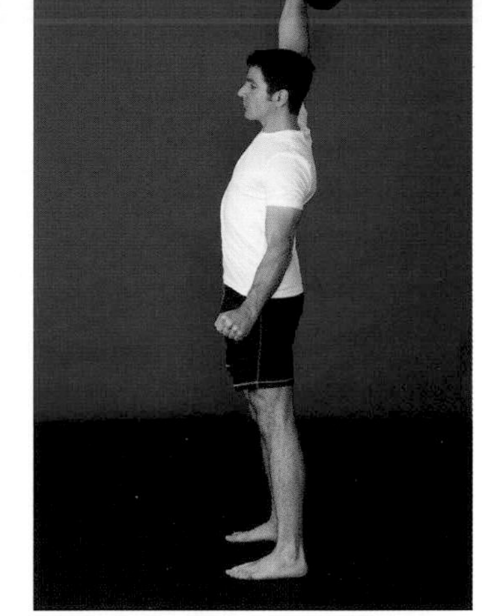

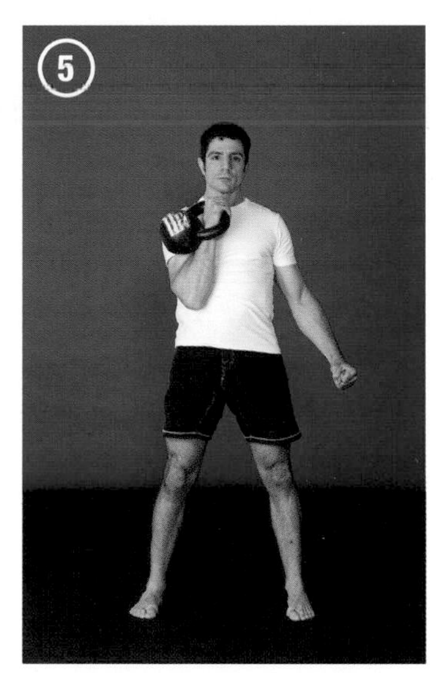

4. At the top of the Military Press, the elbow must be locked completely straight and the bell must be behind you. These two things generate maximum range of motion out of your shoulder and allow your skeleton to hold the load rather than your muscles. At the same time, the lat must pull the shoulder down into the socket to stabilize it..

5. Actively pull the bell back into the rack position with control; you should be using your lats. Do not simply relax and let gravity do the work for you. Complete five reps on the right, then Swing Switch to the left hand and do five reps to balance out the exercise.

THE KOSSACK

The Goblet Squat works on a vertical axis to develop proper squat technique while building hip and groin flexibility as well as leg strength. The Kossack switches to a horizontal axis and increases groin, hamstring and Achilles tendon flexibility as well as core stability. Groin and hamstring flexibility are invaluable qualities for any kicking or ground-fighting martial artist who wants to kick higher or be more mobile on the ground.

Many people have an imbalance between strength and flexibility. If you are strong, you are most likely stiff; if you are flexible, you are probably weak. Without specific effort to balance these two qualities, few people are naturally strong *and* flexible. Imbalances are part of life as a human. We have a dominant hand, a dominant eye, etc. Exercises that improve your strength and flexibility strive for balance and are a necessary part of your training. The Kossack is an exercise that will help you achieve this balance.

You should elevate your hips as little as possible while switching sides; do your best to stay low. Keeping your hips as low as possible throughout the exercise will be more challenging and will develop greater range of motion in the hips and groin. You will also get better results in the strength and range of motion in your upper body. Like every exercise that pushes your range-of-motion limits, use your natural flexibility limits and any discomfort as your guide. Also, be certain to keep your chest tall throughout the movement to increase your spinal strength and flexibility.

Improved groin and hamstring flexibility will increase your kicking height.

The Kossack

Gentlemen: 16 kg / Ladies: 8 kg

1. Raise the kettlebell up like you did for the Goblet Squat.

2. Spread your feet to double shoulder-width apart.

3. Lower yourself to one foot with your bent-side elbow coming to rest inside the bent-side knee. Keep the foot of the bent leg flat on the ground, and open that hip so your knee tracks over your toes. (You can use the elbow that is inside your bent leg to lever against the knee and keep it in line with but not past the toe.) Elongate the other leg straight with its heel on the ground and toes to the sky.

4. Keep your hips as low as possible and your chest as vertical as possible as you switch from side to side.

5. Repeat the same position on the other side.

6. Switch sides 10 times and then lower the bell in front of you at the end of your set. Once the bell is on the ground, sit back onto the ground and shake your legs out before standing back up.

THE WINDMILL

The Windmill is perhaps best described as yoga with weight and exemplifies the hard-style emphasis on matching flexibility with strength as mentioned above in the Kossack. If you have too much of one or the other, the body is off-balance and will deliver a subpar performance on game day because it cannot tap into its fullest potential.

The Windmill is a grind that gives a powerful stretch in the ribs, glutes and hamstrings while at the same time requiring strength and flexibility from the spine and the loaded shoulder. Similar to the TGU, the Windmill is another method to develop increased stability at odd angles. This increased overall range of motion blended with the strength developed through the Windmill will work further toward striking that all-important balance between strength and flexibility. Training that balances the body is essential for improving your general health.

Strength and stability at odd angles can be of great help in the standing clinch to off-balance your opponent while maintaining your balance.

THE WINDMILL

Let me remind you that you're not interested in getting the biggest weight overhead. The kettlebell is the tool, and even with a 16 kg, you will make tremendous strength, flexibility and cardio gains. Please be sure to move in the prescribed pattern only. Do not lean away from the bell because this will center the stretch on your ribs only. Focus on pushing your loaded hip backward to spread the stretch across the loaded-side ribs, glute and hamstring. Also, remember to maintain the lock in the loaded knee to increase the hamstring stretch.

Do not lean away from the kettlebell.

Do not bend the loaded-side leg.

The Windmill

Gentlemen: 16 kg / Ladies: 8 kg

1. Clean the kettlebell to the rack.

2. Use a Military Press to get the bell up into the overhead lockout. Be sure the wrist is locked straight in good punching position and the elbow of the loaded arm is locked straight throughout the entire duration of the exercise.

3. Pivoting on your heels, point your toes away from the loaded side of your body at about a 45-degree angle.

4. With the back of your empty hand on the inside of your thigh, keep your loaded-side leg locked straight, and begin gradually pushing the loaded hip backwards.

5. Keep the loaded-side leg locked straight, and continue pushing the loaded hip backward while you bend sideways away from the loaded hip. Open your chest forward so your shoulders stay aligned vertically. The knee of the unloaded leg can bend while you lower your torso, but if you can keep both legs straight, you will get more of a hamstring stretch. Do not lean away from the weight but rather hinge underneath it.

6. Continue pushing your loaded hip back while opening your chest forward and sliding your empty hand down in the direction of your the floor. Take your time and move with control because there are no extra points for finishing quickly. If your hand reaches the floor, great. If not, don't force it. Just go as far as you can with good form, and use any discomfort and limited range of motion as your guide.

7. When rising, come up briskly by using your lat to "shut your ribs" or shrink the space you just put in between the loaded-side ribs as you went down into the stretch. This will aid in stabilizing the shoulder as you come back up. When moving a weight overhead at this angle, shoulder stabilization is paramount.

8. Finish back in the overhead lockout position in which you started. Lower the bell to the rack with control, and switch hands with a Swing Switch. Alternate sides of the body, and complete three reps on each side.

THE HOT POTATO

The Hot Potato is a great exercise for developing close-range power delivery. Just like the Clean, the Hot Potato will create a virtual shield around your body from the upper-body tension required to perform this exercise. Increased physical durability in the fight game is a good thing.

As the name implies, the Hot Potato is simply bouncing the kettlebell back and forth between your hands. This bounce is not a catch with one hand and then a lob to the other hand that catches and then lobs it back. You must make this bounce quick. It is literally like your hands are two paddles that slap the kettlebell between each other. Sounds simple, but the entire time the kettlebell is bouncing back and forth, your body needs to be in a full HSL. Any relaxation at all will dissipate the force delivered to the bell, so stay locked!

Close-range power can be used to break your opponent's posture.

Although it looks simple and its name is self-explanatory, the details of the Hot Potato require considerable attention for proper execution. If you come from a bodybuilding background, you might be frustrated that years of biceps curls and triceps extensions are not exercises in the hard-style curriculum. Rest assured the screaming fatigue in your pecs will make the Hot Potato a pleasant reminder of days gone by, all the while delivering the benefits of hard-style kettlebell training.

THE HOT POTATO

There is a tendency to want to drop the bell when a round of Hot Potato is completed. Resist the temptation. The preferred method for placing the bell back on the ground is always with control as outlined earlier; do not drop it. If you are training on sand or grass and can drop the bell without harming the bell or the ground and you are intent on doing so, just be sure to watch your feet. Grass will grow back. Toes do not.

"In Shape" vs. "Competition Shape"

If you've competed in any sporting activity, you know the difference between being "in shape" for general fitness and being in "competition shape" for sports. Being in shape is having reached an acceptable level of general fitness. Falling within the most basic health parameters for your age, weight, height, etc., which might keep your doctor from giving you a lecture, is not good enough. Being in shape is important for every human and essential for every athlete.

Competition shape, however, is a different animal altogether. It is unfair and unsafe to require or expect your body to be in competition shape indefinitely. Competitions have set dates, are registered for, and can and should be prepared for so the body is at peak physicality at the time of required performance. However, this doesn't mean that you should balloon up during the off times and need to cut 50 pounds to make your weight division. Keep your cut within reach. Requiring too much from your body on a regular basis will eventually lead to diminished returns. In essence, maintain general fitness year-round and schedule your training so you peak for your competitions.

The Hot Potato

Gentlemen: 16 kg / Ladies: 8 kg

1. Grasp the handle with your thumb facing forward.

2. With a slight swinging motion, bring the bell up and catch the body of the kettlebell in your other hand. Hit your HSL.

3. With the handle facing the ground and perpendicular to your body, toss the bell back and forth between your hands for 30 seconds. When 30 seconds is up, catch the body of the kettlebell with one hand, grip the handle with the other and place it safely on the ground.

THE SNATCH

Often termed the "gold standard," the Snatch is the premier ballistic exercise in the hard-style system. The 2HSW is the fundamental ballistic that teaches everything you need to know about developing the inertia needed to move the bell explosively with the hips. The 2HSW also introduces you to the impressive cardiovascular benefits of hard-style ballistics that will directly transfer to your martial arts training. However, the Snatch takes ballistic training to a whole new, and entirely humbling, level. It requires high levels of strength, stamina and flexibility, thus making the Snatch one of the most demanding exercises technically and physically.

The Snatch is an impressive cardiovascular conditioning-building tool. My good friend Kenneth Jay has studied and written a book on the use of high-speed Snatches for improving maximal oxygen uptake, or VO2 Max. The VO2 Max protocol, as outlined in his book *Viking Warrior Conditioning* uses the hard-style Snatch as the exercise of choice. Suffice it to say, the cardiovascular improvements you will make doing high-rep, high-speed Snatches are impressive.

The Snatch moves the bell from between the legs to the overhead lockout in one smooth, uninterrupted motion. Sounds, easy right? It is for a few reps, but there's a reason it's still the primary physical test exercise for RKC certification: The Snatch requires a multitude of skill sets in order to be performed safely for reps. Heck, anyone can do a Snatch or two, but when done for reps (RKC certification requires 100 reps with the 24 kg bell in five minutes) or speed (VO2 Max), the Snatch requires a thorough understanding of an assortment of skills. For example, you must repeatedly execute HSL full-body tension, proper Face-the-Wall-Squat/Deadlift loading technique, 2HSW maximum hip explosion and the tamed arc of a Clean. You also need TGU shoulder strength and flexibility, a consistent overhead lockout such as the Military Press, and serious stamina. Without all these details dialed in, the Snatch will deteriorate into an unsafe training experience destined for injury in very short order. Again, learn the exercises thoroughly before pushing your physical limits with the Snatch. As always, be smarter than the kettlebell.

THE SNATCH

No matter what your combat sport of choice is, the Snatch will take your cardio through the roof.

The Snatch

Gentlemen: 16 kg / Ladies: 8 kg

(Continued)

1. With the bell's handle parallel to your body, stand behind it as if you are setting up for a One-Handed Swing.

2. Keeping the empty hand off your thigh, initiate a back swing as for a One-Handed Swing.

3. Move the bell forward by firing your hips and hitting your HSL, and just like a Clean "zip up your jacket." (Be certain the bell travels vertically. Snatches that follow the arc of a Swing require your shoulder to stabilize a load moving backward rather than upward. This places undue stress on your shoulder and lower back.)

4. When the bell reaches head height, begin to punch vertically through the handle. This will land the bell gently on your forearm in the overhead lockout. The timing of the bell landing overhead should synchronize with your elbow locking and the rest of your HSL firing. Everything should happen together. There are no bits and pieces in an uncoordinated mess.

The Snatch *(Continued)*

5. To lower the bell, pull it down to the rack in a "corkscrew" fashion.

6. Do not stop in the rack, but pass through it and continue lowering the bell just like you did for the Clean.

7. Pull yourself explosively back and down like you did for the other ballistics you have learned. Allow the bell to move behind you and then fire the hips again. Complete 10 reps. Perform a Swing Switch, and do 10 reps on the opposite side.

The two most common problems people have when learning the Snatch are a "partial press" and an "unstable lockout." Both are easy fixes with some repetition. A partial press means you have not Snatched the bell high enough and need to finish the upward movement with a Press. This is the Snatch, not the Military Press. Give it more juice! It'll get up there if you're not shy about it. Second, the unstable lockout means you're probably not taming the arc like you learned to do with the Clean. Think of a Snatch as a Clean that ends in the overhead lockout rather than the rack. If you treat the Snatch like a Clean rather than like a One-Handed Swing, you'll find your arc will be more vertical and your lockout will be more stable because of the vertical trajectory.

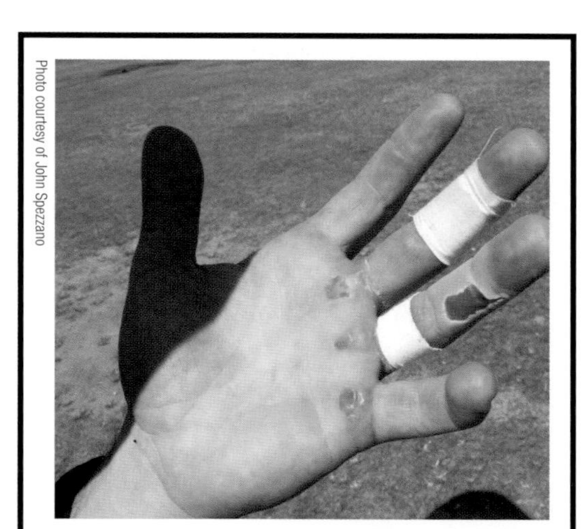

Photo courtesy of John Spezzano

The kettlebell can really beat up your hands. If necessary, use a sock glove to protect them.

One additional safety note when training one-handed ballistics, and the Snatch in particular, is to be aware of the condition of your skin. Each Snatch rep moves the kettlebell from near the floor to overhead at arm's length. This is essentially the maximum distance you can move an object without throwing it, and the price is calculated on the palms of your hands. Initial wear and tear will generate blisters. Be sure to not let them rip open. If a blister forms, stop training and let it heal for a few days. Once the blisters heal and the skin toughens, you will begin developing calluses. This is better than blisters, but calluses require care. If you let them get too large, they will want to get a divorce from your hand and run away with the kettlebell—by that I mean tear off. Use whatever means possible to keep your calluses under control: nail clipper, emery board, etc. Torn skin takes much longer to heal than a blister.

If your skin is taking a long time to get accustomed to kettlebells and is hindering your ability to push your training forward, you can use a "sock glove." The sock glove is a popular choice for hand preservation among kettlebellers. Simply cut the top off a standard athletic sock and discard the foot part. Slip the top of the sock, or "glove," over your fingers so it covers your palm and the area at the base of your fingers that develops the largest calluses. The sock glove works quite well, and it's considerably thinner than a weightlifting glove, so you can still comfortably grip the sizeable handle of the kettlebell. I've seen some people cut a thumb hole in their sock gloves to get it on deeper and keep it in place better. It's really personal preference.

How to Rest

With this much material, you are bound to start pushing your physical limits. Just remember, safety is no accident. Some good rules of thumb to live uninjured by are to always leave one good rep in the tank and never work to the point of complete exhaustion. There's a difference between being tired and being exhausted. Being tired is a normal byproduct of hard training, while being exhausted is when you've pushed your body too far and you cannot safely execute the exercise at hand. Exhaustion means bad form. Bad form means increased risk of injury. *Stop!*

When you do rest, it should be done by one of two methods. The first is active rest, which means shadowboxing or some similar full-body movement that is not too taxing. The second is the Cobra Stretch. If you have just finished some cardio-heavy training, you don't want to stop moving completely. That's when you use the active rest to let your heart rate lower more gradually. This bears repeating: Do not stop moving when your heart rate is high. If you stop moving with an elevated heart rate, you are asking your heart to work unnecessarily hard to circulate your blood. Shadowbox, or walk around moving both your arms and legs. This movement helps your heart circulate blood, allowing your heart rate to come down gradually. Use the Cobra Stretch any time your heart rate is not high.

Cobra Stretch

- Put your hips on the ground.
- Place your hands under your shoulders.
- Keep your elbows straight.
- Fire your lats, pulling your shoulders away from your ears.
- Feel free to emphasize one hip for a few seconds, then switch to the other.

Shorthand Cheat Sheet No. 2	
Goblet Squat	GOB
One-Handed Swing	1HSW
Swing Switch	SWSW
Clean	CL
Military Press	MP
Kossack	KK
Windmill	WM
Hot Potato	HP
Snatch	SN

CHAPTER 4

The Missing Links

"People don't overtrain, they under recover."

—Someone really smart

So far, I have shown you physical training methods to apply in the gym. If applied with the proper mind-set, they will deliver the strength, flexibility and cardio results you seek. However, your work is not only in the gym. Many things you do (or do *not* do) outside the gym can limit your potential and lead to diminished returns in your training. Huh? Let me elaborate.

How many hours a week do you train? Let's say you're a full-time competitor. If so, you probably train about four hours per day for five or six days a week. That's 24 hours per week of training. Sounds like a lot, right? It is. But how many hours are in the week? The answer is: 168. If you subtract nine hours per night for sleep, that brings it down to 105 available hours. If you minus another 24 for your training, then you have a whopping 81 hours left over. That is a lot of time! In fact, it is more than triple your actual training time. You need to understand that what you do in your downtime is equally as important as what you do in the gym.

The above calculations are for a full-time competitor. If you're not a professional fighter, you have even more time than that left over in the week to completely ruin the hard work you did in the gym by eating junk food and staying up late playing video games. With that in mind, let's take a look at three incredibly important factors that will make or break your efforts toward improvement: recovery, nutrition and hydration.

Photo courtesy of Shawn Williams

Reaching your fullest potential is more readily done with proper physical recovery.

The Gym Jones Method

Allowing the body to recover from hard training is vital to reaching peak performance. Peak performance is something the folks at Gym Jones, the elite training facility in Salt Lake City, know a thing or two about. World-class athletes from Brazilian jiu-jitsu, golf, football, luge and cycling, to name a few, come to Gym Jones from places far and wide to improve their already stellar track record. The gym gained fame getting the actors and stuntmen for the movie *300* into camera-ready shape, but long before that, the gym's mastermind, Mark Twight, was using the fitness research he now teaches to keep himself alive.

Twight is one of the greatest alpinists in recent history. He's battle-tested his fitness curriculum while climbing to the top of the world's most perilous mountains in the gutsiest manner imaginable. How do I define gutsy? Well, I don't know about you, but a 60-hour, nonstop (as in no sleep) ascent of Mount McKinley with nothing more than a rope, a climbing partner, water and some energy gel for sustenance qualifies as pretty gutsy to me. That mountain is hard enough to climb with plenty of gear and rest! This is but a snapshot of the types of challenges Twight gave himself as an alpinist. In his own words, "When I began climbing hard, I figured I wouldn't live past 26." 'Nuff said. Outliving his prediction, Twight is now in his 40s and, in my opinion, a teacher with few, if any, peers. He has combined the invaluable information collected from his climbs with his extensive research into strength training, nutrition and physical recovery. I have included some of his wisdom in this chapter.

RECOVERY

I have a student who is very talented but refuses to slow down his training. He pushes it every day, doing multiple training sessions per day. At present, he is suffering from tendinitis in his Achilles tendon and has finally been forced, through injury, to let his body rest from the intensity of his training. He's not alone. This is actually a common occurrence for people who train with frequency and intensity. The question is why? The answer is the quote at the beginning of the chapter. "People don't overtrain, they under recover." Intense physical output requires sufficient physical recovery to allow the body to improve its physical capacity. Your training results *and* subsequent performance will consistently fall short if you continually under-recover.

Let's start by expanding on that statement about "under-recovery." Many athletes push the limits of their training for extended durations. What happens? I know that from my own personal experiences, I would reach a point after a few months of high-intensity training at which I desperately needed some downtime from training. Worse yet, many of my friends would often sustain an injury of some kind in training before their competition even happened. Those repercussions are terrible, but the most devastating and subversive aspect of insufficient recovery is that your training simply hits a point of diminishing returns. This keeps you from reaching your fullest potential. You can work really hard in the gym, but if you don't take the time to recover properly, you're doing more work and risking greater injury in order to reach your goals. Instead, the optimal training routine is maximal results gained through minimal time expenditure. This does not mean training should be easy. Rather, it is intense and focused on the goal, and it also minimizes the risk of injury and follows the essential science of recovery.

There are many tools to help the body recover from training. Gym Jones breaks its recovery tools down into daily, monthly and long-term time frames. The single most important daily tool is to get sufficient sleep at night. Without it, you will not be able to perform at your best. Period. Experiment with eight or nine hours per night, and see which works better for you. You'll be amazed at how much better you feel in general and, equally important, how much better your training goes.

Second only to adequate sleep is a post-workout recovery. When the heart rate is elevated from high-intensity training, the demands for blood circulation are very high. Simultaneously moving your arms and legs while in this state is an "active cool-down" that eases the burden on the heart to circulate the blood. Low-impact methods such as walking, stationary cycling and rowing are safe for your body and strongly preferred to static stretching, which will not help the heart circulate the blood. Flushing the muscles of the toxins built up during training is accomplished in the following manner. Keep a leisurely pace for four to five minutes and then increase to near full output for five to 10 seconds. Repeat this cycle for 20 minutes.

Sleep Cycles

Have you ever noticed that some nights you get less sleep than you think you need but that you actually feel completely rested on waking? Then other nights when you get a lot of sleep, you are still exhausted when you open your eyes. The answer is in your sleep cycle.

According to my friends at Gym Jones, people fall into one of two basic sleep cycles that are either 60 or 90 minutes in duration. During the course of the night, you go through this 60- or 90-minute cycle continuously, alternating between rapid eye movement (REM) sleep, when dreams occur, and non-REM sleep. If you wake up rested, then you've woken up at the end of one of your natural 60- or 90-minute sleep cycles. If you wake up exhausted, then that means on those particular days, you've woken up somewhere in the middle of a sleep cycle that didn't have a chance to be completed.

If waking up tired is a common occurrence, experiment with adjusting the length of your night's sleep to either eight or nine hours. These times will synchronize you with both the 60- and 90-minute cycles, respectively, one of which will leave you noticeably more rested than the other. Try them both. See which one works best for you, then use it. If you get tuned into your sleep cycle and how much sleep you require, you won't need your alarm clock for long. You'll wake up without it.

Another great daily recovery option is the "contrast" shower. The contrast shower alternates between hot and cold water and, in my opinion, is as intense as just about anything I've experienced. I have found incredibly creative ways to curse Mark Twight's name while recovering in the shower from an intense training session. The alternating hot and cold water dilates and constricts the blood vessels in the muscles, which effectively forces post-training toxins out of the muscle tissue.

The recipe for a good contrast shower is as follows. Hang out under the hot water for three to five minutes, massaging the muscles to aid dilation of the blood vessels. Feels great, right? Now comes the hard part: Dial down the temp until it's *all* cold—that means no warm water, folks, and I mean none. Don't be a baby. Just crank it all the way over to the cold and deal with it. If you can handle three to five minutes under the cold, your toughness will not be questioned. After three to five minutes, turn the water back to warm until your body heats up again. Repeat the cycle three times, finishing with cold. As difficult as it can be at first, the feeling you get after a thorough contrast shower is amazing. You will be happy you did it.

If you have the capability, another outstanding daily recovery tool is an ice bath. As a martial artist, your fitness requirements are vast, so your kettlebell training will vary from week to week or even day to day. Some sessions will be more leg intensive while others will focus more on your grip, and other days could be a full-body workout. Similar, but more concentrated than the contrast shower, an ice bath is preferably done immediately after training. Also, it will deliver better results if focused on the part of your body that has done the bulk of the work. For example, if your training was heavy on the legs, as in a lot of Goblet Squats and Kossacks, your legs are what need to recover the most, so let them. There is no need to put your entire body under water unless necessary. Either way, just like the contrast shower, get in the ice bath for five or six minutes and get it over with. No one said you had to enjoy it.

If you do not have access to an ice bath or can't bring yourself to turn the shower down to cold, two other daily recovery tools are the foam roller and going for a walk. If you're not familiar with the foam roller, it is essentially a self-massager that you can use to loosen up hard-worked muscles in your back and legs. They cost about $15, and I can tell you honestly that I use mine every single day. Get one. You can also take a nice walk with the dog or family and get your body moving. Your dog will like it and so will your muscles. Just to be clear, you can use any and all these recovery tools on a daily basis as often as you can work them into your schedule. The more seriously you take your recovery, the better results you will get from your training.

The last daily recovery tool I'll discuss is feeding your depleted muscles immediately after training. The Gym Jones recovery method that I've outlined so far recommends 16 ounces of water and a small snack in a 3:1 or 4:1 ratio of carbs to protein. This snack must be eaten within 20 to 30 minutes after training for optimal results. I recommend you find a calorie counter, and use it to make a snack in the proper ratio because too much protein will reduce the snack's effectiveness. A quick online search will deliver many choices for such a counter. Some are even downloadable to your phone. Interchangeable with a solid snack are recovery drinks that are readily available on the market. These drinks provide this necessary carb-to-protein ratio and are a convenient method to get an accurate ratio of nutrients, especially when your math skills might be as exhausted as your body after hard training. Do a little research and find one that works for you. In the absence of such a drink, chocolate milk is a great choice. Just be sure to use low-fat milk, and if you buy it pre-mixed, do your best to skip the ones that use high-fructose corn syrup.

Monthly recovery tools include massage and acupuncture. A good massage therapist is priceless. I get a massage every week, and it is incredible how much of a difference I feel when I miss a few weeks because of schedule conflicts. The parts just don't work together as well as they do when I get a regular massage. Also, just like your training, be sure to change the style of massage you receive after a few months. Your body will definitely have acclimated. For myself, I cycle between Thai massage and deep-tissue. These types of massages are both intense but in different ways, switching from one to the other surprises the body. Keep in mind that you are using massage here as a monthly tool for recovery and not to rehab a specific injury. If you have sustained an injury, be certain to get it properly diagnosed and treated by a qualified health-care professional.

Acupuncture is one of the oldest forms of medicine in the world used to promote health and balance in the body. With a 2,000-year history, acupuncturists know many ways to help your health. Though it is also quite useful for specific health problems, it is acupuncture's pre-emptive nature of keeping you from getting ill in the first place that makes it an effective recovery tool. I first tried acupuncture 15 years ago and have experienced terrific results for a host of issues, including stubborn tendinitis that seemed to never get better. If you haven't tried acupuncture, get a recommendation from a friend or qualified professional and give it a go.

For long-term recovery, consider a seasonal approach to your martial art. Generally, martial arts don't have seasons like in baseball or football, but that doesn't mean you can't give yourself a yearly schedule with an "offseason" to do something else. Just have that "something else" be somewhat physically related to the physical output of your martial art of choice. For example, if you're a Brazilian jiu-jitsu competitor, don't become a cyclist in the "offseason." This would require you to change your body's strengths and the duration of your physical output too greatly. Stick to something that is still based on bursts of energy.

Another great long-term recovery option is a vacation. I know many of us, me included, forgo this because of financial and time restrictions. The restorative qualities of time with no, or at least fewer, responsibilities are not to be underestimated. For example, while working on this book, my wife and I went on a much-needed vacation to New Zealand. This was an outstanding way to physically recharge through some continuous days of rest and relaxation. Find a way to get a week or two off during the year and spend it with family or friends. You will be glad you did.

One final long-term recovery tool is Rolfing, also known as Structural Integration. There is a layer of connective tissue underneath the skin that wraps around the muscles and separates them from each other while providing them with support and protection. This layer is known as fascia, and it provides a structure to the muscles of your body. Over time, this layer can be compromised by poor movement patterns and can lead to sub-optimal performance in competition and training. Rolfing, or Structural Integration, is a method of therapeutic bodywork through massage that reorganizes your fascia back to its original shape. This allows the body to take on its more natural structural posture. Rolfing works on the place where imbalances first arise and often makes future massage, chiropractic and acupuncture treatments more effective.

These are some suggestions for how to structure your recovery from daily tools to those you use less often. The variety will give you choices on the method, but the end result is that you find a way to help your body recover from training. Without recovery, you will hinder your improvement. If you have any concerns about any of these methods, of course consult your doctor before attempting them.

The key factors that directly affect your ability to recover from intense training are diet, sleep, rest and stress. Read the section on nutrition to learn more about diet, but otherwise, let's just agree there are many outstanding dietary plans to choose from. Poor diet choices will harm your improvement. Do a little trial-and-error research to find a diet that gives you enough calories to train intensely and without getting fat. You already know how important sleep is to peak physical performance, but I'll repeat it again: Get enough sleep! Rest is different from sleep. Rest means taking your downtime as actual downtime. Focus your high physical output on the task at hand, which is your training. If you enjoy high-energy pastimes, don't do them when you're preparing for a specific event. Lastly, stress is undeniably taxing on the body. To gain the most out of your training and to perform at your best, do whatever you can to reduce stress, wherever it occurs in your life, work, relationships, etc.

The best sign that you are recovering well is if your performance in training gets better. What if it's not? How do you know whether your diet is off or you're not sleeping, resting and/or reducing your stress? Follow the evidence. If you're training your butt off and you're getting fat or closely resemble a guy on a hunger strike, something's wrong with your diet. Perhaps you wake up exhausted, then something's off with your sleep habits.

Maybe you don't have a frame of reference for when you're exhausted. If so, one objective test you can use is to track your waking or resting heart rate. Your waking heart rate is just that, the heart rate you greet the day with. If your alarm clock jolts you out of bed, perhaps this is not the best test for you. The resting heart rate is taken when you are not doing anything active, perhaps while sitting at your desk. If your waking/resting heart rate is elevated, you're not recovering sufficiently. Another sign of negative impact on your recovery is going to bed later and sleeping less.

Once you've followed the evidence, adjust your recovery with the variety of tools now at your disposal. Then retest your heart rate and/or evaluate your sleep issues for a few days and see whether you've remedied the problem. If not, keep making adjustments until proof of sufficient recovery is evident.

NUTRITION

Just like insufficient recovery leads to diminishing returns on your performance, your level of general fitness can only be as good as the fuel you put in the system. If you want the Ferrari to perform, you'd better not fill it up with low test. The exact same principle applies to the human body. No matter which dietary protocol you choose to follow, the more whole, organically produced food you take in, the better. Skip highly processed and fast foods as much as possible. If you're unsure what I mean by "highly processed," here's a test: If your lunch comes out of plastic wrap and contains ingredients you can't pronounce, chuck it.

Marty Gallagher, the author of *The Purposeful Primitive,* outlines two general approaches to timing your caloric intake, which refers to when to eat during the day. These two schedules are diametrically opposed to each other, and there are proponents who swear by both methods. The specifics of *what* you eat notwithstanding, these two schedules are pretty standard for those on a strength-building regimen. The first is to eat multiple small meals throughout the course of the day. This is known in some circles as the Parrillo Diet and is popular among bodybuilding competitors who know a lot about how to decrease body fat and gain muscle mass. The second is to eat one big meal at the end of the day, which is known as the Warrior Diet. Ori Hofmekler, author of *The Warrior Diet*, claims numerous health and fitness advantages from the diet's "intermittent fasting." These two radically different approaches to timing your caloric intake are both popular. The fact that they can coexist is clear evidence that there is not just one way.

Whichever approach you think sounds good, don't forget about quality. As one of my first instructors said so eloquently while choking down a Ding Dong, "It's better to eat crap than to eat nothing at all." Well, yes. I suppose that's undeniable. However, it's also better to eat good food than crap. Produce treated with pesticides and livestock that are given hormones for growth will pass those materials on to you when they're on your plate. Be certain your meals are made from whole, organic foods whenever possible.

Fast/junk food is one of the quickest ways to damage your training results.

In terms of specific diet plans, there are many to choose from. Everything from "tree-hugger vegan" to "caveman paleo" exist, and both are widely popular. What you eat is up to you, but it should be based on what makes your body change in the manner desired. However, don't forget food is also meant to be enjoyed, so it ought to taste good as well as fuel the machine. This book is not a cookbook, but a happy medium can and should be found between a healthy, beneficial diet and good-tasting food. If it doesn't taste good, it will be harder to convince yourself it's worth the trouble, no matter how good it is for you.

You will find a method that works for you, but you must do so with this caveat: It has to work for the duration. By duration, I mean the rest of your life and not just your competition years because those years

Or you can use a lighter kettlebell if you have one. Here is a solution if you are already using the lightest of the weights. Take the cap off a half-full plastic water bottle, balance it right-side up on the knuckles of your fist and perform the TGU without spilling the water. It's not heavy, but it's plenty challenging.

Bottoms-Up TGU

Gentlemen: 16 kg / Ladies: 8 kg

(Continued)

1. Pull and roll.

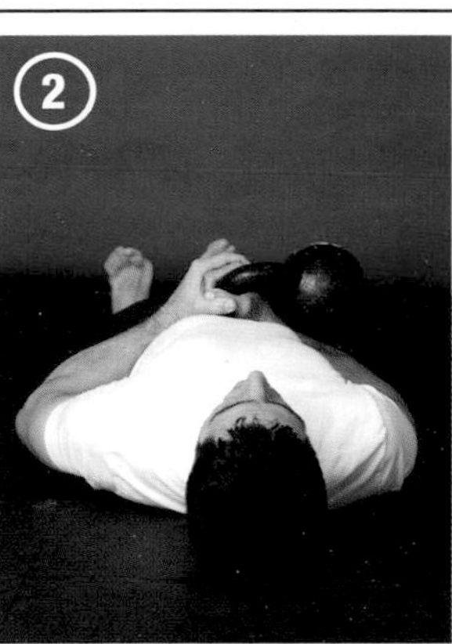

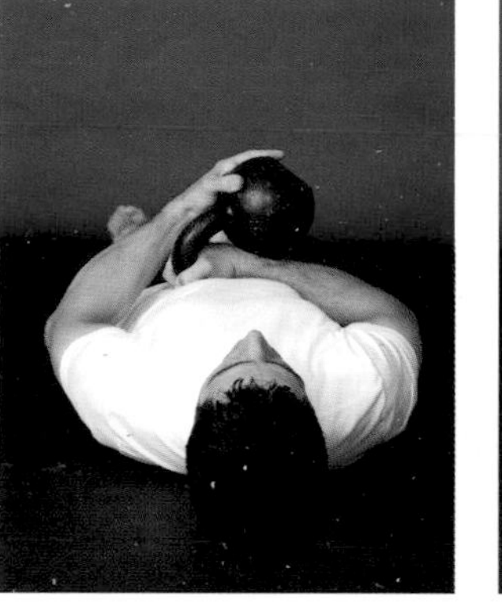

2. Keep the kettlebell low and close to your body as you adjust it to the bottoms-up position. .

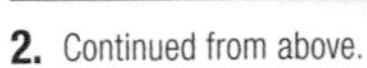

2. Continued from above.

3. Crush the handle.

4. Move to the firing-range position.

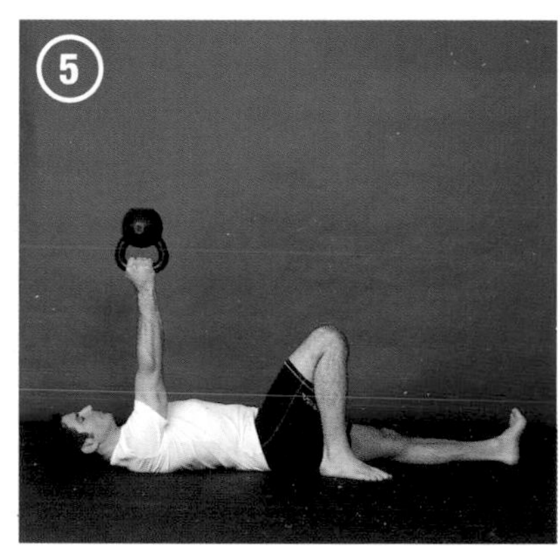

5. Adjust yourself to the hand-and-foot position.

Double-Bell Military Press

Gentlemen: (2) 16 kg bells / Ladies: (2) 8 kg bells

1. Perform a Double-Bell Clean.

2. With the bells in the rack, narrow your stance back to standard issue.

3. From the rack position, press both bells up to the overhead-lockout position.

4. Pull the bells back to the rack.

5. Repeat. Perform sets of five reps. Presses are a burner, so be sure to get plenty of rest in between. Be certain to widen your stance before placing the bells safely back on the ground.

I haven't seen a lot of people do this type of press and would venture to say it's pretty rare. Kenneth Jay calls the Double-Bell Military Press with both kettlebells in one hand something of a "stupid human trick," and I can see how one might apply a certain circus sideshow aspect to them. However, the grip strength required to stabilize two kettlebell handles with a single hand is a legitimate training benefit. Crushing your grip around one handle gives outstanding results, as you've already seen, but crushing two handles that you can't fully close your hand around adds a new dimension to your grip strength. That's not to mention the added weight going overhead and the increased stability required for the greater asymmetrical load.

However, before you can press both bells, you have to rack them, and this can be a bit awkward with both bells in one hand. The best way to do it is by performing a "Safety Clean." This is essentially just swinging the bells from between your legs up to the rack. Keep your thumb facing away from you, and allow the bells to travel in an upward and diagonal arc to the loaded side. This will let them land softly in the rack. Once the bells are in the rack, be sure they are centered over each other. Because they are stacked, only one bell can rest on your forearm. The other bell is balancing on top, and it can get squirrely when moving from the rack to overhead. You might be using odd-size kettlebells for this press. Perhaps you do not have two bells of equal size or you are working up in weight. If so, it will be easier to balance the smaller bell on the top. Then fire all the tension you have at your disposal and press them up and overhead. Does it matter whether they get to the full overhead lockout? Nope. If you can only go up four inches with good form, go up four inches. Eventually, you will get all the way to the lockout.

Double-Bell Military Press (One Hand)

Gentlemen: (2) 16 kg bells / Ladies: (2) 8 kg bells

1. Grasp both bells in one hand with your thumb facing forward.

2. Hike the bells back

3. Execute a "Safety Clean" to get them to the rack.

4. Crush the handles and white-knuckle your other hand.

5. Press them up and overhead. Repeat three times, then switch sides to balance out.

Shorthand Cheat Sheet No. 3	
Catch-and-Release Two-Handed Swing	CnR2HSW
Catch-and-Release One-Handed Swing	CnR1HSW
Squat Clean	SQCL
One-Handed Swing With Vertical Flip	1HSWFlip
One-Handed Swing With Horizontal Spin	1HSWSpin
Bottoms-Up Clean	BUCL
Bottoms-Up Military Press	BUMP
Bottoms-Up Windmill	BUWM
Bottoms-Up Turkish Get Up	BUTGU
One-Legged Deadlift (Bent Leg)	1LDLBent
One-Legged Deadlift (Straight Leg)	1LDLStraight
Double-Bell Deadlift	DBDL
Double-Bell Swing	DBSW
Odd-Weight Double-Bell Swing	OWDBSW
Double-Bell Clean	DBCL
Double-Bell Military Press	DBMP
Double-Bell Military Press (One Hand)	DBMP1Hand

CHAPTER 6

Combining the Exercises

If you compete or train in mixed martial arts, you work with a lot of tools—punches, kicks, knees, elbows, takedowns, takedown defenses, submissions and submission defenses to name a few. You probably isolate these aspects of your training to a degree, but sooner or later, you've got to put them together at the same time. If you don't, you will have prepared very poorly for the cage. The same is true for the hard-style kettlebell exercises you now know. You've learned the exercises individually, and that is important for the learning process. However, combining them into compound-training routines will work wonders for your results.

Also, aside from being a great way to keep you working on a variety of exercises, compound-training routines allow you to balance your training in nearly every session. If you cycle through a good variety of exercises in the course of your workout, you will undoubtedly touch on some of your strengths and your weaknesses. Certain routines will focus more on ballistics to increase your cardiovascular conditioning. Other routines that are grind based will build raw power and odd-angle strength. You can also create routines that do equal parts of both. If you only do Swings or TGUs, your training will be lopsided and sooner than later stagnate. Don't forget how the body acclimates. Keep it fresh by regularly switching up your training routines.

Be sure your training time is long enough to include a full-body warm-up, well-rounded training with the kettlebell itself and a good cool-down, as well. Emphasize joint mobility and range of motion, especially in the shoulders, hips and knees in your warm-up. Be certain you don't jump into your high-intensity training while cold. Once you do start the actual training, keep it high-intensity and focused on the details. Then be certain to cool down appropriately, as defined in Chapter 4 on recovery.

Some of the following routines in this chapter are done for a specific amount of time, others for reps. If, for example, the routine calls for "2HSW x 20," then you do 20 reps of Two-Handed Swings. If it says "DBSW x 30 seconds," then you do Double-Bell Swings for 30 seconds. Either way, these recommended reps/times are just a framework; they are not written in stone. If you are crushing it, push yourself further. However, if you are gassing, remember to always be smarter than the kettlebell. If you begin to feel your skin blister, stop immediately. Unless an exercise is marked "naked" or with an otherwise specified weight, all of the following routines are designed for a man to use the 16 kg bell and a woman to use the 8 kg. If you are up to the task of using a larger bell feel free, but do it with perfect form.

I've given you a lot of exercises in this book to facilitate well-balanced training. Are there more exercises out there? Absolutely. Do you need them? Absolutely not. However, don't be afraid to continue your research, but do it when you have trained this book's material to the point that you *need* to find something else. Use this book to develop rock-solid fundamentals, then press ahead.

Enjoy!

PROGRAM MINIMUM (WITH NAKED TGU)

Two-Handed Swing, Naked Turkish Get Up

Fundamental—Repeat sequence 2 times.

- 2HSW x 30 Seconds
- Naked TGU x 1 (Right Hand)
- 2HSW x 30 Seconds
- Naked TGU x 1 (Left Hand)

Transitional—Repeat sequence 2 times.

- 2HSW x 45 Seconds
- Double-Up Naked TGU x 1 (Right Hand)
- 2HSW x 45 Seconds
- Double-Up Naked TGU x 1 (Left Hand)

Complex—Repeat sequence 3 times.

- 2HSW x 60 Seconds
- Triple-Up Naked TGU x 1 (Right Hand)
- 2HSW x 60 Seconds
- Triple-Up Naked TGU x 1 (Left Hand)

TWO-HANDED SWING

NAKED TURKISH GET UP

PROGRAM MINIMUM WITH LOAD

Two-Handed Swing, Turkish Get Up

Fundamental—Repeat sequence 2 times.

- 2HSW x 30 Seconds
- TGU x 1 (Right Hand)
- 2HSW x 30 Seconds
- TGU x 1 (Left Hand)

Transitional—Repeat sequence 3 times.

- 2HSW x 45 Seconds
- TGU x 1 (Right Hand)
- 2HSW x 45 Seconds
- TGU x 1 (Left Hand)

Complex—Repeat sequence 3 times.

- 2HSW x 60 Seconds
- DUTGU x 1 (Right Hand)
- 2HSW x 60 Seconds
- DUTGU x 1 (Left Hand)

TWO-HANDED SWING

TURKISH GET UP

STABILISTIC

Snatch, One-Legged Deadlift (Bent Leg), Two-Handed Swing, Hot Potato

SNATCH

Fundamental—Repeat entire sequence 5 times.

- SN x 10 (Right Hand)
- SWSW x 1
- SN x 10 (Left Hand)
- Naked 1LDL x 5 (Right Leg)
- Naked 1LDL x 5 (Left Leg)
- 2HSW x 20
- HP x 20
- Active Rest x 30 Seconds

TWO-HANDED SWING

Transitional—Repeat entire sequence 5 times.

- SN x 12 (Right Hand)
- SWSW x 1
- SN x 12 (Left Hand)
- 1LDL x 5 (Right Leg)
- 1LDL x 5 (Left Leg)
- 2HSW x 25
- HP x 25
- Active Rest x 30 Seconds

Complex—Repeat entire sequence 5 times.

- SN x 15 (Right Hand)
- SWSW x 1
- SN x 15 (Left Hand)
- 1LDL x 5 (Right Leg)
- 1LDL x 5 (Left Leg)
- 2HSW x 35
- HP x 40
- Active Rest x 30 Seconds

HOT POTATO

ONE-LEGGED DEADLIFT (BENT LEG)

THE SOPRANOS

Squat Clean, Kossack, Goblet Squat, Hot Potato

Fundamental—Repeat entire sequence 5 times.

- SQCL x 5
- GOB x 5
- HP x 10
- KK x 5
- SQCL x 5
- Active Rest x 30 Seconds

Transitional—Repeat entire sequence 5 times.

- SQCL x 10
- GOB x 10
- HP x 20
- KK x 10
- SQCL x 10
- Active Rest x 20 Seconds

Complex—Repeat entire sequence 5 times.

- SQCL x 15
- GOB x 12
- HP x 30
- KK x 12
- SQCL x 15
- Active Rest x 10 Seconds

SQUAT CLEAN

KOSSACK

GOBLET SQUAT

HOT POTATO

GRIP CRUSHER

Snatch, Bottoms-Up Clean, Bottoms-Up Military Press, Bottoms-Up Windmill

Fundamental—Repeat entire sequence 2 times.

- SN x 5 (Right Hand)
- BUCL x 1 (Right Hand)
- BUMP x 1 (Right Hand)
- BUWM x 1 (Right Hand)
- SWSW x 1
- SN x 5 (Left Hand)
- BUCL x 1 (Left Hand)
- BUMP x 1 (Left Hand)
- BUWM x 1 (Left Hand)
- SWSW x 1
- Active Rest x 30 Seconds

Transitional—Repeat entire sequence 2 times.

- SN x 7 (Right Hand)
- BUCL x 1 (Right Hand)
- BUMP x 2 (Right Hand)
- BUWM x 1 (Right Hand)
- SWSW x 1
- SN x 7 (Left Hand)
- BUCL x 1 (Left Hand)
- BUMP x 2 (Left Hand)
- BUWM x 1 (Left Hand)
- Active Rest x 30 Seconds

Complex— Repeat entire sequence 3 times.

- SN x 10 (Right Hand)
- BUCL x 2 (Right Hand)
- BUMP x 3 (Right Hand)
- BUWM x 1 (Right Hand)
- SWSW x 1
- SN x 10 (Left Hand)
- BUCL x 2 (Left Hand)
- BUMP x 3 (Left Hand)
- BUWM x 1 (Left Hand)
- Active Rest x 30 Seconds

SNATCH

BOTTOMS-UP CLEAN

BOTTOMS-UP MILITARY PRESS

BOTTOMS-UP WINDMILL

HIGH FLYIN'

Two-Handed Swing, Squat Clean, Catch-and-Release One-Handed Swing, One-Handed Swing With Vertical Flip, One-Handed Swing With Horizontal Spin, Snatch

Fundamental—Repeat entire sequence 3 times.

- 2HSW x 5
- SQCL x 5
- CnR1HSW x 5 (Right Hand)
- SWSW x 1
- CnR1HSW x 5 (Left Hand)
- SWSW x 1
- SN x 5 (Right Hand)
- SWSW x 1
- SN x 5 (Left Hand)
- Active Rest x 60 Seconds

TWO-HANDED SWING

SQUAT CLEAN

Transitional—Repeat entire sequence 3 times.

- 2HSW x 10
- SQCL x 10
- CnR1HSW x 5 (Right Hand)
- SWSW x 1
- CnR1HSW x 5 (Left Hand)
- SWSW x 1
- 1HSWFlip x 3 (Right Hand)
- SWSW x 1
- 1HSWFlip x 3 (Left Hand)
- SWSW x 1
- SN x 15 (Right Hand)
- SWSW x 1
- SN x 15 (Left Hand)
- Active Rest x 60 Seconds

(Continued)

ONE-HANDED SWING WITH VERTICAL FLIP

CATCH-AND-RELEASE ONE-HANDED SWING

High Flyin' *(Continued)*

Complex—Repeat entire sequence 3 times.

- 2HSW x 10
- SQCL x 10
- CnR1HSW x 5 (Right Hand)
- SWSW x 1
- CnR1HSW x 5 (Left Hand)
- SWSW x 1
- 1HSWFlip x 5 (Right Hand)
- SWSW x 1
- 1HSWFlip x 5 (Left Hand)
- SWSW x 1
- 1HSWSpin x 1 (Right Hand)
- SWSW x 1
- 1HSWSpin x 1 (Left Hand)
- SWSW x 1
- SN x 10 (Right Hand)
- SWSW x 1
- SN x 10 (Left Hand)
- Active Rest x 45 Seconds

ONE-HANDED SWING WITH HORIZONTAL SPIN

SNATCH

DOUBLE-BELL NO. 1

Double-Bell Deadlift, Double-Bell Swing

Foundational—Repeat entire sequence 5 times.

- DBDL x 10
- Active Rest x 30 Seconds
- DBSW x 10
- Active Rest x 30 Seconds

Transitional—Repeat entire sequence 7 times.

- DBDL x 15
- Active Rest x 20 Seconds
- DBSW x 15
- Active Rest x 20 Seconds

Complex – Repeat entire sequence 10 times.

- DBDL x 15
- Active Rest x 10 Seconds
- DBSW x 20
- Active Rest x 10 Seconds

DOUBLE-BELL DEADLIFT

DOUBLE-BELL SWING

DOUBLE-BELL NO. 2

Double-Bell Swing, Odd-Weight Double Bell Swing (Gentlemen: [2] 16 kg bells and another bell of a different size / Ladies: [2] 8 kg bells and another of a different size)

Foundational—Repeat entire sequence 3 times.

- DBSW x 20 Seconds
- Active Rest x 40 Seconds
- OWDBSW x 20 Seconds
- Active Rest x 40 Seconds
- OWDBSW (Switch Bells to Opposite Hands) x 20 Seconds
- Active Rest x 40 Seconds

Transitional—Repeat entire sequence 3 times.

- DBSW x 30 Seconds
- Active Rest x 30 Seconds
- OWDBSW x 30 Seconds
- Active Rest x 30 Seconds
- OWDBSW (Switch Bells to Opposite Hands) x 30 Seconds
- Active Rest x 30 Seconds

Complex—Repeat entire sequence 3 times.

- DBSW x 45 Seconds
- Active Rest x 15 Seconds
- OWDBSW x 45 Seconds
- Active Rest x 15 Seconds
- OWDBSW (Switch Bells to Opposite Hands) x 45 Seconds
- Active Rest x 15 Seconds

DOUBLE-BELL SWING

ODD-WEIGHT DOUBLE-BELL SWING

DOUBLE-BELL NO. 3

Double-Bell Swing, Double-Bell Clean, Double-Bell Military Press (Gentlemen: [2] 16 kg bells / Ladies: [2] 8 kg bells)

Foundational—Repeat entire sequence 15 times.

- DBSW x 1
- DBCL x 1
- DBMP x 1

Transitional—Repeat entire sequence 15 times.

- DBSW x 5
- DBCL x 1
- DBMP x 3
- Active Rest x 30 Seconds

Complex—Repeat entire sequence 15 times.

- DBSW x 10
- DBCL x 3
- DBMP x 5
- Active Rest x 15 Seconds

DOUBLE-BELL SWING

DOUBLE-BELL CLEAN

DOUBLE-BELL MILITARY PRESS

CHAPTER 7

Hybrid Training

"Under pressure you will not rise to the occasion; you will sink to the level of your training."

— Barrett Tillman

Adrenaline is a hormone released by the adrenal gland under threat of physical violence (real or imagined) that, among other things, increases the heart rate and opens the blood vessels. "Hybrid training" uses kettlebell exercises to induce a similar physically fatigued state in which to train. Working out in a fatigued state can improve your performance under the effects of adrenaline, such as during a competition or an actual self-defense scenario.

Like Tillman's quote implies, the body responds differently when adrenalized than it does in the gym. If you've sparred hard in the gym and also fought in the ring, you know that they are two very different animals. This is mainly because of the effects of adrenaline that you are under when in a real fight vs. the comfort of the gym. If you practice poorly without adrenaline flowing, your response when under pressure will be even worse. Getting your block knocked off is a true possibility in the cage or ring, and the adrenaline that goes along with that reality is something you have to handle. Luckily, you can program yourself to accept and work through a highly adrenalized state. This is exactly what the following hybrid-training drills are all about.

Here's the plan; it's simple yet devious. Use kettlebell exercises in long enough duration to raise the heart rate and begin taxing the muscular and cardiovascular systems, then do various application aspects of your training—footwork, empty-handed striking, sticks, etc. I'll get you started with some suggestions. Then let your imagination guide you.

FOOTWORK DRILLS

Footwork is an essential skill regardless of what your combative sport of choice may be—no matter whether you're a boxer, muay Thai practitioner, *savate* competitor, MMA fighter, or Greco-Roman or freestyle wrestler. Any martial art that spends time in an upright position needs to use good footwork. If you already possess decent footwork skills, then please feel free to improvise. If you are new to standing mobility, then peruse the following choices and find something that strikes your fancy.

In jeet kune do, the foundational linear footwork pattern is the "step and slide." The step and slide is a common pattern in many martial arts, but for those of you unfamiliar with it, I'll break it down. Assume a left- or right-lead stance. Step first with the foot that is closest to the direction you want to move. Step with your lead foot to move forward, then simply slide the other foot on the ground up so you return to your proper stance width. To step back, start with your rear foot and slide your lead foot back to end in your proper stance width. Do not step your feet past each other, like you do when walking normally. If you start in a left lead, you should end in a left lead.

Good footwork will get you out of harm's way.

Another basic linear-footwork pattern is the "push shuffle." The push-shuffle pattern uses the opposite foot to push your body where you'd like to go and your feet finish in proper stance width. To move forward, your rear foot pushes you in that direction. To move backward, your lead foot pushes you back in that direction. It's pretty straightforward, and to the naked eye, the step and slide and push shuffle may look the same, but they feel very different.

Both those patterns move you in a straight line. To add circular movement into the mix, square your feet up at shoulder width, similar to your stance for the Face-the-Wall Squat. Shuffle in a circle to the right or left. Change directions frequently and efficiently, using as little time to change as possible. Take a few minutes to practice these footwork patterns independently and in conjunction with the others.

For those of you who train Philippine martial arts, I have included a sidebar with three versions of triangular footwork: female, male and lateral triangles. Be sure to have single or double sticks in hand while performing these choices.

OK, now that we're clear on some basic footwork, here's the first hybrid-training routine. You will use kettlebell Swings to increase your heart rate and then work your footwork skill set while winded. Once you complete your Swings, do not rest. Piggyback immediately off the cardio output from the Swings with the footwork drills. Make sure you continue to shadowbox while you work the pattern of choice. This will aid your training and simultaneously act as an active rest from the high intensity of the swings.

HYBRID TRAINING NO. 1: FOOTWORK

Two-Handed Swing, Linear Footwork Patterns, Circular Footwork Patterns

Foundational—Repeat entire sequence 2 times.

- 2HSW x 30 Seconds
- Step and Slide (Forward, Backward, Left and Right) x 30 Seconds
- 2HSW x 30 Seconds
- Push Shuffle (Forward, Backward, Left and Right) x 30 Seconds
- 2HSW x 30 Seconds
- Circular Footwork (Left and Right) x 30 Seconds
- Active Rest x 60 Seconds

Transitional—Repeat entire sequence 3 times.

- 2HSW x 45 Seconds
- All Footwork Variations x 30 Seconds
- 2HSW x 45 Seconds
- All Footwork Variations x 60 Seconds
- Active Rest x 60 Seconds

Complex—Repeat entire sequence 3 times.

- 2HSW x 60 Seconds
- All Footwork Variations x 30 Seconds
- 2HSW x 45 Seconds
- All Footwork Variations x 45 Seconds
- Active Rest x 60 Seconds

TWO-HANDED SWING

Triangular Footwork

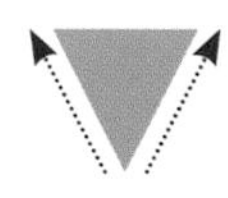

Advancing Female Triangle:
Start with your feet together on the bottom point. Step to the upper left corner of the triangle with your left foot. Bring your feet back together at the bottom point. Step to the upper right corner with your right foot. Bring your feet back together at the bottom point and repeat.

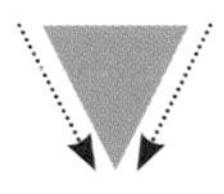

Retreating Female Triangle:
Start with your feet shoulder-width apart. Keep your right foot stationary, and step to the third point of the triangle behind you with your left foot. Bring your right foot back to where it started. Now step with your right foot to the rear point of the triangle. Return to the original position and repeat.

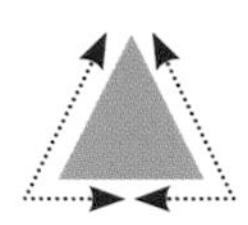

Advancing Male Triangle:
With your feet at the bottom two points of the triangle, bring your right foot to your left foot and continue it to the forward point of the triangle. Reverse the movement back to your original position. Now move your left foot to your right foot and continue it onto the forward point. Return to the original position and repeat.

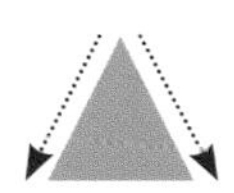

Retreating Male Triangle:
With both feet on the forward point, keep your right foot stationary and step your left foot back to the rear left corner. Bring your left foot back to where it started, and now move your right foot back to the rear right corner. Come back to the original position and repeat.

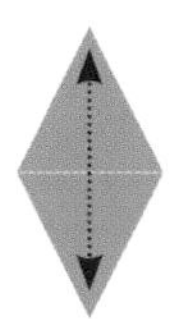

Lateral Triangle:
Place your left foot on the left corner where the triangles meet and keep it stationary. Place your right foot on the forward point, and step it back and forth between the forward and rear points of the triangle. To switch which foot moves, just stop and reset to the right side of the triangle, and keep your right foot stationary while moving your left forward and back.

HEAVY-BAG PUNCHING DRILLS

Being able to strike with good form is easy when it's round one and you're fresh. However, like everything else, form deteriorates as fatigue sets in. Before you know it, your hands are down by your chest, leaving your head wide open for your opponent to punch. Perhaps you start throwing slow, telegraphed, sloppy kicks that are easy to counter. Worse still is getting tired when kneeing in the clinch. Exhaustion leaves you defenseless against your opponent's knee strikes and an easy target to off-balance for throwing or takedowns. Learning how to shore up these weaknesses with good form when you're tired is definitely an ace up your sleeve.

Before starting any of these drills, get some colored tape that will be visible on your heavy bag. Place a piece of tape to mark the nose, chin, right side of the head, left side of the head, right side ribs/elbow, left side ribs/elbow, stomach, right-side quad and left-side quad. You don't have to start with this many targets, but accuracy counts, so make sure you force yourself to hit where you intend to hit. Improvising a combination is fine, but when you hit, you have to hit the mark. Give yourself realistic targeting and make your shots count.

Photo by Rick Hustead

Punches that have power when you're tired are a must.

The principle we used of alternating swings with attribute training from the footwork drill is the same format for these rounds with the heavy bag. I have isolated punches, knees, elbows and kicks into separate training routines. You can and should eventually mix the striking tools into the same round, but at first, keep it simple. Perform the kettlebell exercises for the specified amount of time or reps, then do the bag drill for the specified amount of time. For those of you who punch and kick hand-held pads and/or kick shields but do not use a heavy bag, don't worry. Have your training partner ready with the necessary gear for you to hit after your swings. Even better, the two of you can alternate the training rounds and act as good motivators for each other. Motivation is often easier with a partner than when alone.

The exercises in this section are designed to tax your cardiovascular system, replicate your standing-guard position and wear down your upper-body strength. Developing these three elements through fatigue will strengthen your game as well as your body. Set your timer for three-minute rounds with one-minute rest periods. When the timer rings, remember to do active rest between rounds. Do not sit/lie down and stop moving when your heart rate is elevated from high-intensity training.

Unless your hands are conditioned to hit without hand wraps, never punch the bag hard when your hands are not wrapped. Without the proper hand conditioning, you are courting injury. Because wrapped hands make kettlebell training difficult, use your boxing gloves (14 ounces or bigger) during these rounds rather than bag gloves. Boxing gloves will give you more protection and compensate somewhat for the lack of wraps. Either way, you don't have to hit hard. Just hit a lot and hit the mark! Gradually increase your pace and intensity while hitting the bag as the rounds progress. Sometimes hit quickly, but insert pauses in the combos. Sometimes hit a little slower but nonstop. Sometimes hit quickly and nonstop. You get the idea. Be sure to incorporate the footwork drills you ingrained previously during and between your combos.

HYBRID TRAINING NO. 2: PUNCHING

Two-Handed Swing, Clean, Military Press

Foundational—Repeat entire sequence 2 times.

- 2HSW x 60 Seconds
- Punch the Heavy Bag x 60 Seconds
- 2HSW x 30 Seconds
- Punch the Heavy Bag x 30 Seconds
- Active Rest x 60 Seconds

TWO-HANDED SWING

Transitional—Repeat entire sequence 3 times.

- 2HSW x 60 Seconds
- Punch the Heavy Bag x 60 Seconds
- 2HSW x 30 Seconds
- Punch the Heavy Bag x 30 Seconds
- Active Rest x 60 Seconds
- CL x 30 Seconds (Right Hand)
- SWSW x 1
- CL x 30 Seconds (Left Hand)
- Punch the Heavy Bag x 60 Seconds
- CL x 15 Seconds (Right Hand)
- SWSW x 1
- CL x 15 Seconds (Left Hand)
- Punch the Heavy Bag x 30 Seconds
- Active Rest x 60 Seconds

CLEAN

Complex—Repeat entire sequence 2 times.

- 2HSW x 60 Seconds
- Punch the Heavy Bag x 60 Seconds
- 2HSW x 30 Seconds
- Punch the Heavy Bag x 30 Seconds
- Active Rest x 60 Seconds
- CL x 30 Seconds (Right Hand)
- SWSW x 1
- CL x 30 Seconds (Left Hand)
- Punch the Heavy Bag x 60 Seconds
- CL x 15 Seconds (Right Hand)
- SWSW
- CL x 15 Seconds (Left Hand)

(Continued)

MILITARY PRESS

Hybrid Training No. 2: Punching *(Continued)*

- Punch the Heavy Bag x 30 Seconds
- Active Rest x 60 Seconds
- CL, CL, CL, MP x 60 Seconds (Switch Hands After Every MP)
- Punch the Heavy Bag x 60 Seconds
- CL, CL, CL, MP x 30 Seconds (Switch Hands After Every MP)
- Punch the Heavy Bag x 30 Seconds
- Active Rest x 60 Seconds

HEAVY-BAG KICKING DRILLS

Depending on the system, kicks are delivered with the shin, heel, toe, top of the foot, sole of the foot; you name it. There are plenty of specific weapon choices, but they're all attached to the leg. The improved cardio uptake you will experience with the following exercises will be gained through specific and extensive lower-body output. As you tire from this output, you will need to use better form while kicking, otherwise you won't finish the round. Proper form will make you efficient and dangerous even when tired. Set your timer for three-minute rounds with one-minute rest period. When the timer rings, remember to do active rest between rounds. Do not sit/lie down and stop moving when your heart rate is high.

You can throw any kind of kick you like, just kick! Similar to the punching workout, have your kicking pace start gradually and build in intensity as the rounds progress. Sometimes hit hard, but insert pauses in the combos. Sometimes hit light but nonstop. Sometimes hit hard and nonstop. Moving the legs is much more work than moving the arms, so don't be surprised if you're gassing more than with the punching version. Remember, those marks are on the bag for a reason. Hit them. Use the footwork drills you learned previously during and between your combos.

Photo by Rick Hustead

Letting your hips do the work will deliver power even when you're getting tired.

HYBRID TRAINING NO. 3: KICKING

Two-Handed Swing, Squat Clean, Kossack, One-Legged Deadlift (Bent Leg)

Foundational—Repeat entire sequence 3 times.

- 2HSW x 30 Seconds
- Kick the Bag x 30 Seconds
- SQCL x 30 Seconds
- Kick the Bag x 30 Seconds
- KK x 30 Seconds
- Kick the Bag x 30 Seconds
- Active Rest x 60 Seconds

Transitional—Repeat entire sequence 3 times.

- 2HSW x 30 Seconds
- KK x 30 Seconds
- Kick the Bag x 30 Seconds
- 2HSW x 30 Seconds
- SQCL x 30 Seconds
- Kick the Bag x 30 Seconds
- Active Rest x 60 Seconds

(Continued)

TWO-HANDED SWING

SQUAT CLEAN

Hybrid Training No. 3: Kicking *(Continued)*

Complex—Repeat entire sequence 4 times.

- 2HSW x 30 Seconds
- 1LDLBent x 30 Seconds (Alternate Legs on Each Rep)
- Kick the Bag x 30 Seconds

- SQCL x 30 Seconds
- KK x 30 Seconds
- Kick the Bag x 30 Seconds
- Active Rest x 60 Seconds

KOSSACK

ONE-LEGGED DEADLIFT (BENT LEG)

HEAVY-BAG ELBOWING-AND-KNEEING DRILLS

Many striking systems use elbow and knee strikes. In muay Thai, the elbow and knee is used in the clinch and both weapons deliver devastating results. Outside of striking from this position, simply being strong in the clinch can give you a decided advantage over your opponent. Your success or failure at breaking his posture can rapidly put you in the driver's seat. The exercises in this training routine are designed to develop your cardio, your strength at odd angles, your explosive snap in the hips and your tremendous leg strength. Set your timer for three-minute rounds with one-minute rest period.

You can use the curved or straight knee, it's up to you. You can do individual knee strikes or throw them in rapid succession. Whichever you choose to employ, be certain to focus on the tape targets and make your strikes accurate, especially when you're winded. Again, feel free to up the intensity as the round progresses. Program yourself to be able to go hard later into the round. Also, just like the other rounds, sometimes hit hard, but insert pauses in the combos. Sometimes hit light but nonstop. Sometimes hit hard and nonstop.

Photo by Rick Hustead

One well-placed knee strike can easily end the fight.

Photo by Rick Hustead

Elbow strikes are an incredibly effective close-range weapon.

HYBRID TRAINING NO. 4: ELBOWS AND KNEES

Two-Handed Swing, Naked Turkish Get Up, Clean, Goblet Squat

Foundational—Repeat entire sequence 3 times.

- 2HSW x 30 Seconds
- Naked TGU From Lying Down to Standing Position Only x 1 (Right Hand)
- Knee the Bag x 30 Seconds
- 2HSW x 30 Seconds
- Naked TGU From Lying Down to Standing Position Only x 1 (Left Hand)
- Elbow the Bag x 30 Seconds
- Active Rest x 60 Seconds

Transitional—Repeat entire sequence 3 times.

- 2HSW x 30 Seconds
- Naked TGU From Lying Down to Standing Position Only x 1 (Right Hand)
- Elbow the Bag x 30 Seconds
- CL x 10 (Right Hand)
- SWSW x 1
- CL x 10 (Left Hand)
- Naked TGU From Lying Down to Standing Position Only x 1 (Left Hand)
- Knee the Bag x 30 Seconds
- Active Rest x 60 Seconds

TWO-HANDED SWING

Complex—Repeat entire sequence 5 times.

- Naked TGU From Lying Down to Standing Position Only x 1 (Right Hand)
- 2HSW x 15
- GOB x 15
- Knee and Elbow the Bag x 30 Seconds
- Naked TGU From Lying Down to Standing Position Only x 1 (Left Hand)
- CL x 10 (Right Hand)
- SWSW x 1
- CL x 10 (Left Hand)
- Rapid-Fire, Nonstop Knees and Elbows Until the Round Ends
- Active Rest x 60 Seconds

NAKED TURKISH GET UP

CLEAN

GOBLET SQUAT

TAKEDOWN DRILLS

The ability to take an opponent down to the ground gave wrestlers a strong advantage in the early days of MMA competition. Being able to quickly put someone on his back is generally the result of a well-timed and well-executed takedown. This leaves you in the much-preferred dominant top position and your opponent fighting for his life on the bottom. The following exercises are geared toward explosive leg strength and improved core stability.

Set your timer for three-minute rounds with one minute of active rest between rounds. You can use any variation of takedown you like. Head-inside single leg or standard double leg, it doesn't matter which because you're not going to finish the takedown. Instead, you just hit your shot on the heavy bag. Whatever takedown you choose, though, be sure to drop your level and hit your shot like you mean it. Don't slack. Also, just like the last routine, have your pace start gradually and build intensity as the rounds progress. Feel free to use assorted footwork patterns in between and to set up your shot.

Photo by Rick Hustead

Takedowns and takedown defense can guide the fight in your favor.

HYBRID TRAINING NO. 5: TAKEDOWNS

Two-Handed Swing, Goblet Squat, Military Press, Clean, Hot Potato, Bottoms-Up Clean, Bottoms-Up Military Press

TWO-HANDED SWING

Foundational—Repeat entire sequence 3 times.

- 2HSW x 60 Seconds
- Shoot Your Takedown x 30 Seconds
- GOB x 10
- CL x 1 (Right Hand)
- MP x 5 (Right Hand)
- GOB x 10
- CL x 1 (Left Hand)
- MP x 5 (Left Hand)
- Shoot Your Takedown x 30 Seconds
- Active Rest x 60 Seconds

Transitional—Repeat entire sequence 4 times.

- 2HSW x 15
- GOB x 10
- CL x 1 (Right Hand)
- MP x 3 (Right Hand)
- SWSW x 1
- CL x 1 (Left Hand)
- MP x 3 (Left Hand)
- Shoot Your Takedown x 30 Seconds
- HP x 30 Seconds
- BUCL x 15 Seconds (Right Hand)
- SWSW x 1
- BUCL x 15 Seconds (Left Hand)
- Shoot Your Takedown x 30 Seconds
- Active Rest x 60 Seconds

MILITARY PRESS

GOBLET SQUAT

Complex—Repeat entire sequence 4 times.

- 2HSW x 30 Seconds
- BUCL, BUMP x 15 Seconds (Right Hand)
- SWSW x 1
- BUCL, BUMP x 15 Seconds (Left Hand)
- Shoot Your Takedown x 30 Seconds
- 2HSW x 7
- GOB x 7
- CL x 3 (Right Hand)
- MP x 3 (Right Hand)
- SWSW x 1
- CL x 3 (Left Hand)
- MP x 3 (Left Hand)
- Take Your Shot Until the Round Ends
- Active Rest x 60 Seconds

CLEAN

HOT POTATO

BOTTOMS-UP CLEAN

BOTTOMS-UP MILITARY PRESS

WEAPONRY DRILLS

As you know from shadowboxing with the stick, maintaining your grip on the weapon is paramount. Without it, you will find yourself weaponless. The exercises below are designed to develop full-body strength, maximum tension and an extraordinary grip.

You can use two sticks or one and you can perform any kind of stick strike you feel like doing. Just be sure to use the tape marks to target your shots accurately and if you are using a single stick, do at least one round with the stick in your weak hand. Just like the last routine, have your pace start gradually and increase the intensity as the rounds progress. Just like the other training routines, sometimes hit hard but have pauses in the combos or vice versa, etc.

Photo by Rick Hustead

Power and speed with weaponry is great, but it has to last.

Since we're focusing on the stick now, increasing your grip strength is of the utmost importance. Make certain to crush the handle of the bell when holding the HSL at the end of your CL or MP and especially on the bottoms-up material. Gravity never sleeps so don't lose focus!

HYBRID TRAINING NO. 6: STICKS

Two-Handed Swing, Clean, Military Press, Goblet Squat, Squat Clean, Bottoms-Up Clean, Catch-and-Release Two-Handed Swing, Catch-and-Release One-Handed Swing, Bottoms-Up Military Press

Foundational—Repeat entire sequence 2 times.

- 2HSW x 30 Seconds
- CL x 5 (Right Hand)
- MP x 1
- SWSW x 1
- CL x 5 (Left Hand)
- MP x 1
- Hit the Bag x 30 Seconds
- 2HSW x 30 Seconds
- CL x 10 (Right Hand)
- MP x 1
- SWSW x 1
- CL x 10 (Left Hand)
- MP x 1
- Hit the Bag Until the End of the Round
- Active Rest x 60 Seconds

TWO-HANDED SWING

Transitional—Repeat entire sequence 3 times.

- CnR2HSW x 30 Seconds
- CL x 10 (Right Hand)
- MP x 1
- SWSW x 1
- CL x 10 (Left Hand)
- MP x 1
- Hit the Bag x 30 Seconds
- GOB x 10
- SQCL x 5
- BUCL x 5 (Right Hand)
- SWSW x 1
- BUCL x 5 (Left Hand)
- Hit the Bag Until the End of the Round
- Active Rest x 60 Seconds

CLEAN

Complex—Repeat entire sequence 3 times.

- CnR2HSW x 30 Seconds
- BUCL x 5 (Right Hand)
- SWSW x 1
- BUCL x 5 (Left Hand)
- Hit the Bag x 30 Seconds
- CnR1HSW x 15 Seconds (Right Hand)

(Continued)

MILITARY PRESS

GOBLET SQUAT

Hybrid Training No. 6: Sticks *(Continued)*

- BUCL x 1 (Right Hand)
- BUMP x 3 (Right Hand)
- SWSW x 1
- CnR1HSW x 15 Seconds (Left Hand)
- BUCL x 1 (Left Hand)
- BUMP x 3 (Left Hand)
- Hit the Bag Until the End of the Round
- Active Rest x 60 Seconds

SQUAT CLEAN

BOTTOMS-UP CLEAN

CATCH-AND-RELEASE TWO-HANDED SWING

CATCH-AND-RELEASE ONE-HANDED SWING

BOTTOMS-UP MILITARY PRESS

CHAPTER 8

Final Thoughts

Martial arts are a means of self-discovery through a study of combat. Some people climb mountains, others race motorcycles. We kick, punch, wrestle and submit each other. Some days, we kick, punch, wrestle and submit better than other days. The days when we're doing great are easy and deliver the encouragement we need to continue training. It's when we're having an off day that we need to go back to our foundation of a strong mind-set. If you can believe in yourself on an off day, then you can do anything. Believing in yourself is the aspect of martial arts training that is mirrored in your hard-style kettlebell training. When you actually do a kettlebell exercise that you weren't sure you could do, your confidence grows in equal proportion to your doubts diminishing. There is nothing better.

By now you've seen how helpful hard-style kettlebell training can be to your martial arts training and competition as well as how useful it can be for general fitness throughout your life. We've looked at ways to get stronger, more flexible and increase your cardio capacity. Clearly, a lot of work can be done with minimal gear. Most of the exercises were executed using one little kettlebell. We've also explored proper diet and hydration as well as detailed approaches to recovery, which is the all-important factor that will give you the opportunity to reach your fullest potential. Everyone has potential, but talent is potential that has been achieved. Such an achievement is only possible through a lot of dedicated work and is the clearest sign of success in any aspect of your martial arts training or competition.

Finally, I want to genuinely thank you for allowing me to show you these exercises and explain my approach to training. I am an incredibly lucky guy who gets to do what he loves for a living. However, without you, the student, I would not be able to do what I love. Wishing you good, hard and safe training!

RECOMMENDED READING

The truth is this list does not have an end nor should it. Your research must never reach a point at which you can honestly say you know enough. Everything you learn leads you to something new, and if what you learn gets you fired up about training, then make your way through these books. Feel free to keep adding to the list.

Absorb What Is Useful

by Dan Inosanto

Guro Dan Inosanto is "the man" and is undoubtedly the greatest influence on my research, training and teaching. While all his books are excellent, this one is about the essence of training and has always been my favorite.

Enter the Kettlebell!

by Pavel Tsatsouline

Pavel Tsatsouline is one of the pioneers in exposing the West to the fitness tsunami that is the Russian kettlebell. He is the head of the Russian Kettlebell Challenge organization under which I am a certified instructor and has an encyclopedic knowledge of all things fitness. Everyone who uses kettlebells should own this book.

On Combat

by Lt. Col. Dave Grossman

Lt. Col. Dave Grossman is an internationally respected authority on the subject of combat stress. This work in particular looks at the physiology the human body is subjected to in highly adrenalized situations brought on by a physical, life-threatening conflict.

The Purposeful Primitive

by Marty Gallagher

Marty Gallagher is a highly respected lifting coach who has also held numerous titles in powerlifting and Olympic lifting. This book strips away all the unnecessary and leaves you with an essential read for any athlete serious about strength, fat loss and overall fitness.

Viking Warrior Conditioning

by Kenneth Jay

Kenneth Jay is a true encyclopedia of strength and fitness knowledge with a knack for explaining heavy concepts in a digestible manner. If you're into VO2 Max and pushing your training, get your hands on anything Jay puts on the market.

EXERCISE INDEX

BLACK BELT BOOKS

Bruce Lee Books from Black Belt Books

BRUCE LEE: Wisdom for the Way

by Bruce Lee

Wisdom for the Way gives readers direct access to Bruce Lee's thoughts. It pulls from many of Bruce Lee's sources—quotes, pictures, sketches—to create a visually comprehensive reference to the master. The book is also the perfect gift for martial arts enthusiasts, collectors and philosophers who want insight into the mind of Bruce Lee in a compact presentation. 144 full-color pgs. (ISBN-13: 978-0-89750-185-9)

Book Code 491—Retail $15.95

TAO OF JEET KUNE DO

by Bruce Lee

This is Bruce Lee's treatise on his martial art, *jeet kune do*. This international best-seller includes the philosophy of jeet kune do, mental and physical training, martial qualities, attack and strategy. 208 pgs. Size: 8-1/2" x 11" (ISBN-13: 978-0-89750-048-7)

Book Code 401—Retail $16.95

BRUCE LEE'S FIGHTING METHOD: The Complete Edition

by Bruce Lee and M. Uyehara

Bruce Lee's Fighting Method: The Complete Edition brings the iconic four-volume *Fighting Method* series together into one definitive book. Intended as an instructional document to complement Lee's foundational *Tao of Jeet Kune Do*, this restored and enhanced edition of *Fighting Method* breathes new life into hallowed pages with digitally remastered photography and a painstakingly refurbished interior design for improved instructional clarity. This 492-page hard-bound book also includes 900+ digitally enhanced images, newly discovered photographs from Lee's personal files, a new chapter on the Five Ways of Attack penned by famed first-generation student Ted Wong, and an analytical introduction by Shannon Lee that helps readers contextualize the revisions and upgrades implemented for this special presentation of her father's work. 492 pgs. Size 7" x 10". (ISBN-13: 978-0-89750-170-5)

Book Code 494—Retail $34.95

CHINESE GUNG FU: The Philosophical Art of Self-Defense (Revised and Updated)

by Bruce Lee

Black Belt Books' new edition of *Chinese Gung Fu: The Philosophical Art of Self-Defense* gives martial arts enthusiasts and collectors exactly what they want: more Bruce Lee. In addition to the master's insightful explanations on *gung fu*, this sleek book features digitally enhanced photography, previously unpublished pictures with Lee's original handwritten notes, a brand-new front and back cover, and introductions by widow Linda Lee Cadwell and daughter Shannon Lee. Fully illustrated. 112 pgs. (ISBN-13: 978-0-89750-112-5)

Book Code 451—Retail $12.95

To order, call toll-free: (800) 581-5222 or visit www.blackbeltmag.com/shop

Other Books from Black Belt Books

BLACK BELT BOOKS

COMBAT HAPKIDO:
The Martial Art for the Modern Warrior
by John Pellegrini

Combat Hapkido: The Martial Art for the Modern Warrior imparts the wisdom, experience and real-life tactical know-how of grandmaster John Pellegrini. Filled with kicks, strikes and skills that soldiers and civilians have successfully implemented in real-life combat scenarios, this full-color instructional guide gives readers a foundational understanding of this contemporary *hapkido*-inspired martial art.
160 full-color pgs. (ISBN-13: 978-0-89750-181-1)
Book Code 507—Retail $24.95

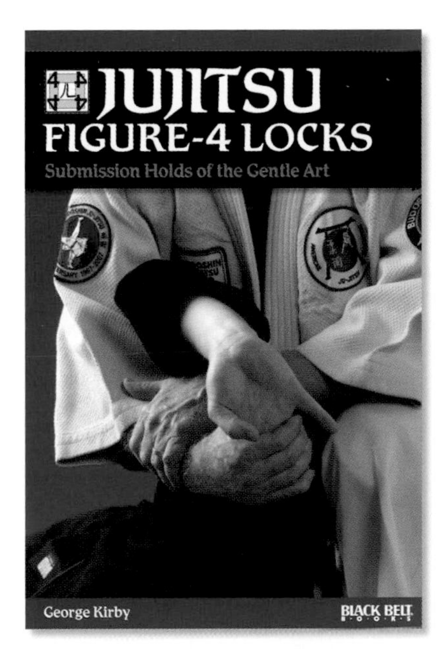

JUJITSU FIGURE-4 LOCKS:
Submission Holds of the Gentle Art
by George Kirby

American Ju-Jitsu Association co-founder George Kirby takes the next step forward with his new book *Jujitsu Figure-4 Locks: Submission Holds of the Gentle Art*. As a continuation of his series from Black Belt Books, the well-respected martial artist continues to document his *jujitsu* evolution and experience for readers of all skill levels. In this book, Kirby focuses on the essential principles of jujitsu's most effective trapping techniques: the figure-4 lock and its variations.
192 pgs. (ISBN-13: 978-0-89750-180-4)
Book Code 506—Retail $18.95

THE FIRST MIXED MARTIAL ART:
Pankration From Myths to Modern Times
by Jim Arvinitis

Jim Arvanitis, internationally known as the "Father of Modern Pankration," presents his brutally effective martial art in *The First Mixed Martial Art: Pankration From Myths to Modern Times*. Arvanitis explores *pankration's* ancient Greek roots, as well as its modern combat and mixed-martial applications. Regardless of individual style, any martial artist will benefit from the strategies and cultural history presented within.
232 full-color pgs. (ISBN-13: 978-0-89750-182-8)
Book Code 508—Retail $24.95

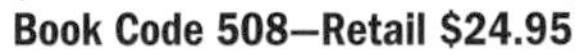

THE GRAPPLER'S HANDBOOK:
Gi and No-Gi Techniques
by Jean Jacques Machado with Jay Zeballos

The Grappler's Handbook: Gi and No-Gi Techniques gives readers an integrated approach to triumphing on the mat. No matter whether the reader is looking to immerse himself in the strategy of Brazilian *jiu-jitsu* or to experience the adrenaline rush of submission grappling or mixed martial arts, Jean Jacques Machado and co-author Jay Zeballos clearly demonstrate how martial artists of all levels can successfully transition between styles. 182 full-color pgs. (ISBN-13: 978-0-89750-183-5)
Book Code 509—Retail $26.95

To order, call toll-free: (800) 581-5222 or visit www.blackbeltmag.com/shop

BLACK BELT MAGAZINE VIDEO

DVDs from Black Belt Magazine Video

REALITY-BASED PERSONAL PROTECTION—SERIES 2

by Jim Wagner

Reality-based self-defense pioneer Sgt. Jim Wagner returns with a new three-DVD series, taking his lessons and tactics to a new level! In *Volume 1: How to Beat Various Fighters*, Wagner breaks down how to train for real-life combat against punchers, kickers, grapplers, etc. In *Volume 2: The Most Important Self-Defense Lesson of Your Life*, Wagner presents 12 techniques essential to prevailing in street-fighting situations, including the one-knee strike, choke escape and open-hand strike, etc., that everyone needs to survive. In *Volume 3: Conflict Conditioning*, Wagner shows you what it takes to stay physically and mentally prepared for all stages of the conflict spectrum. Topics include protecting the box, wall-fight kicking, fight-and-write exercise, hogtie defense, the clinch escape, mind over pain, various push-ups, S.A.S. sit-ups, two-seat person rescue, the *savate* hop and "walking the gauntlet."

Volume 1: How to Beat Various Fighters (Approx. 100 min.) **DVD Code 9719—Retail $29.95**

Volume 2: The Most Important Self-Defense Lesson of Your Life (Approx. 60 min.) **DVD Code 9729—Retail $29.95**

Volume 3: Conflict Conditioning (Approx. 60 min.) **DVD Code 9739—Retail $29.95**

COMBATIVES FOR STREET SURVIVAL

by Kelly McCann

Train to prevail in any street conflict or assault situation with Kelly McCann in this highly anticipated companion-DVD series for his acclaimed book, *Combatives for Street Survival: Hard-Core Countermeasures for High-Risk Situations.* McCann is a combatives instructor and former Marine with more than 25 years of experience in self-defense. He is also the founder of Crucible, a high-risk-environment training provider that serves Department of Defense special-missions units and federal law-enforcement and intelligence agencies. Each disc in this series features a special optional caption track displaying chapters/pages from McCann's book corresponding to the subject matter being discussed on the DVD!

Volume 1: Index Positions, the Guard and Combatives Strikes (Approx. 90 min.) **DVD Code 9779—Retail $29.95**

Volume 2: Weapon Counterattacks and Situational Combatives (Approx. 60 min.) **DVD Code 9789—Retail $29.95**

Volume 3: Contact Training, Protective Equipment and Street Scenarios (Approx. 55 min.) **DVD Code 9799—Retail $29.95**

ULTIMATE CONDITIONING

by Scott Sonnon

International *sambo* coach and renowned martial arts trainer Scott Sonnon presents three martial arts fitness DVDs! *Ultimate Conditioning Volume 1: Strikers, Ultimate Conditioning Volume 2: Ground Fighters and Ultimate Conditioning Volume 3: Kickers* include demonstrations and guided training circuits for a wide and challenging variety of workouts using body weight, sandbags, medicine balls, kettlebells, plyo-boxes and Sonnon's own Clubbell® that are designed to improve strength, endurance and task-specific conditioning for the techniques involved in the particular volume's focus (striking, ground fighting or kicking).

Volume 1: Strikers (Approx. 50 min.) **DVD Code 9749—Retail $29.95**

Volume 2: Ground Fighters (Approx. 52 min.) **DVD Code 9759—Retail $29.95**

Volume 3: Kickers (Approx. 49 min.) **DVD Code 9769—Retail $29.95**

To order, call toll-free: (800) 581-5222 or visit www.blackbeltmag.com/shop

BEYOND KUNG FU:
Breaking an Opponent's Power Through Relaxed Tension

by Leo T. Fong

Beyond Kung Fu: Breaking an Opponent's Power Through Relaxed Tension teaches the reader how to use the subtle power of nonresistance to break an opponent. The book features detailed, step-by-step photo sequences that identify and use relaxed-tension techniques in a street fight, competition or cinematic settings. It also addresses *chi*, meditative- and physical-conditioning exercises, and specific grappling, hitting and kicking attacks. 147 pgs. (ISBN-13: 978-0-89750-179-8)

Book Code 505—Retail $16.95

FIGHT NIGHT!
The Thinking Fan's Guide to Mixed Martial Arts

by Lito Angeles

Fight Night! The Thinking Fan's Guide to Mixed Martial Arts breaks down the essential, bread-and-butter terms and techniques for the MMA fan. Starting with the "Americana choke" and ending with the "wrestling clinch," each entry includes a description of the technique, detailed photo sequences of common applications and educational and entertaining insights. Perfect for loyal followers or viewers new to the arena! 224 full-color pgs. (ISBN-13: 978-0-89750-175-0)

Book Code 501—Retail $29.95

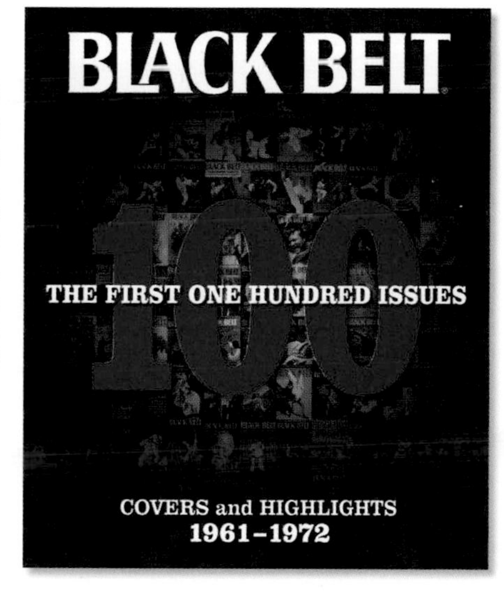

BLACK BELT:
The First 100 Issues

Black Belt: The First 100 Issues (Covers and Highlights 1961-1972) celebrates the genesis of one of the longest-running and most influential sports magazines ever in a large-format, softcover, color coffee-table book. As a commemorative compilation of *Black Belt* magazine's industry-defining material, it features the cover art and content highlights of the first 100 issues. Cover photographs and illustrations include such martial arts luminaries as Bruce Lee, Chuck Norris, Mas Oyama, Joe Lewis, Gene LeBell as well as celebrity practitioners like Sean Connery and Toshiro Mifune. 208 pgs. (ISBN-13: 978-0-89750-173-6)

Book Code 499—Retail $34.95

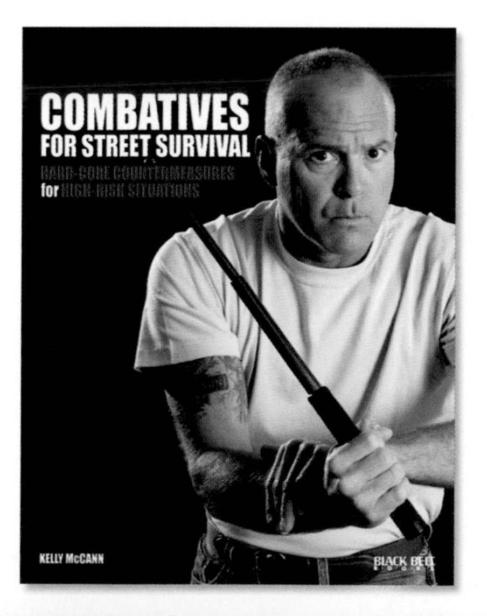

COMBATIVES FOR STREET SURVIVAL:
Hard-Core Countermeasures for High-Risk Situations

by Kelly McCann

In Combatives for Street Survival: Hard-Core Countermeasures for High-Risk Situations, author Kelly McCann leads the reader through simple but powerful and effective methods of self-defense. Based on visceral combatives techniques, the book leads the reader through multilayered scenarios and concepts for empty-hand and weapons self-defense. It will redefine anyone's attitude toward street violence! 192 Pgs. (ISBN-13: 978-0-89750-176-7)

Book Code 502—Retail $24.95

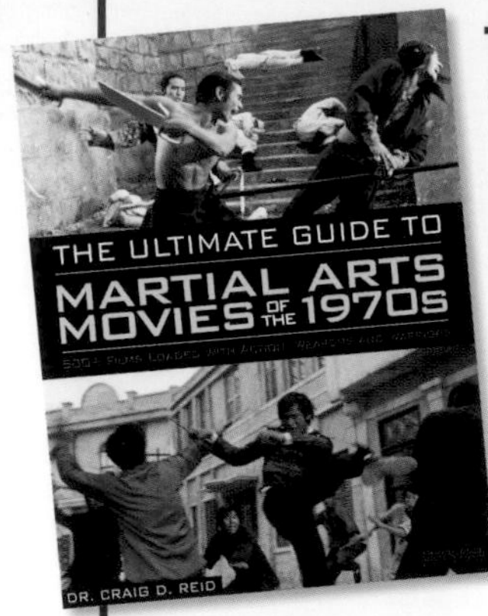

THE ULTIMATE GUIDE TO MARTIAL ARTS MOVIES OF THE 1970s

by Dr. Craig D. Reid

Dive into the decade that brought martial arts cinema to the masses in this epic full-color book by Dr. Craig D. Reid, one of America's most respected martial arts film historians and critics! This dynamic guide launches into "martialogies" of 500-plus films loaded with action, weapons and warriors! Each entry is filled with humor and contains a concise plot summary, behind-the-scenes reel (and real) history, fight statistics, insights into martial arts choreography and styles, and other surprising factoids about each title. Includes a complete index listing more than 2,000 actors and movies by all their English variations, as well as an index for movies by country of origin. 288 pgs. (ISBN-13: 978-0-89750-192-7)

Book Code 497—Retail $26.95

THE ULTIMATE GUIDE TO JEET KUNE DO

by the Editors of Black Belt

The Ultimate Guide to Jeet Kune Do gives insight into the intriguing martial art of Bruce Lee. The art's most successful students interpret the evolution and originator through a collection of articles from the Black Belt archives. Features articles by, profiles of and lessons from the following martial artists: Dan Inosanto, Tim Tackett, Bob Bremer, Jerry Poteet, Paul Vunak, James DeMile, Gary Dill, James Lee, Jerry Beasley and Richard Bustillo. 147 pgs. (ISBN-13: 978-0-89750-186-6)

Book Code 510—Retail $24.95

THE ULTIMATE GUIDE TO BRAZILIAN JIU-JITSU

by the Editors of Black Belt

The Ultimate Guide to Brazilian Jiu-Jitsu follows the evolution of this seemingly unstoppable art from an unorthodox interpretation of traditional *jujutsu* to the most dominant position in the grappling world. Spanning two decades of material from the *Black Belt* archives, the book features interviews with Gracie legends, instructions on how to execute the art's brutally efficient techniques and illustrations of iconic BJJ fighters demonstrating essential grappling moves. *The Ultimate Guide to Brazilian Jiu-Jitsu* is the definitive resource on the modern world's most impressive martial art. 191 pgs. (ISBN-13: 978-0-89750-171-2)

Book Code 498—Retail $16.95

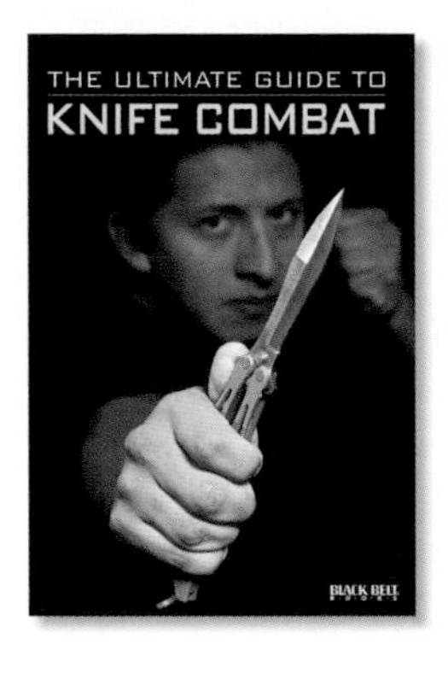

THE ULTIMATE GUIDE TO KNIFE COMBAT

by the Editors of Black Belt

More effective than a fist and more accessible than a gun, the knife is the most pragmatic self-defense tool. *The Ultimate Guide to Knife Combat* celebrates this simple, versatile, sometimes controversial weapon with essays and instructional articles written by the world's foremost experts, including Ernest Emerson, Hank Hayes, Jim Wagner and David E. Steele. *The Ultimate Guide to Knife Combat* presents an international cross-section of knife cultures and styles—from the heroic legacy of America's bowie knife to the lethal techniques of the *kukri*-wielding Gurkhas of Nepal—and features essential empty-hand techniques, exercises to improve your fighting skills, and advice on choosing the knife that's right for you. Spanning two decades of material from the *Black Belt* archives, *The Ultimate Guide to Knife Combat* provides everything you need to know about fighting with or against a blade. 312 pgs. (ISBN-13: 978-0-89750-158-3)

Book Code 487—Retail $16.95

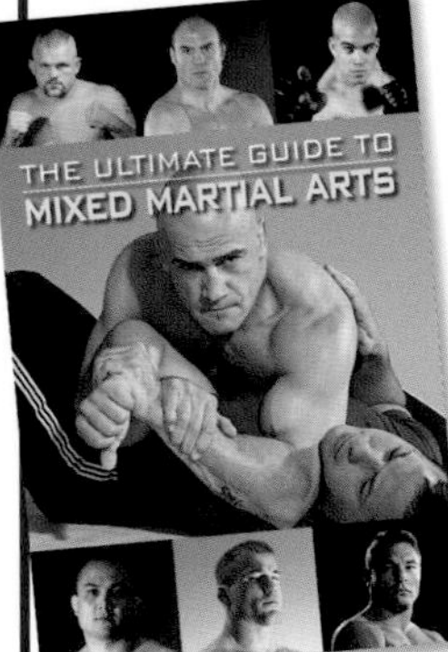

THE ULTIMATE GUIDE TO MIXED MARTIAL ARTS

by the Editors of Black Belt

Only one sport has reinforced elbow smashes to the head, flying knees and liver kicks. From MMA's controversial inception to its mainstream acceptance, from the iconic legacy of Rickson Gracie to the freakish knockout power of Chuck Liddell, from the unstoppable determination of Randy Couture to the emergence of tomorrow's champions, *Black Belt* has covered the sport's genesis and evolution. With *The Ultimate Guide to Mixed Martial Arts*, you will leap into the octagon with Chuck Liddell, experience the artery-crushing chokes of Rickson Gracie, devour Randy Couture's prescription for peak performance, master Dan Henderson's winning training methods and suffer the nasty takedowns of UFC bad-boy Tito Ortiz. A compilation of instructional articles and interviews with the industry's greatest champions, *The Ultimate Guide to Mixed Martial Arts* is the definitive resource on the athletes and techniques of the world's most intense and popular new sport. 216 pgs. (ISBN-13: 978-0-89750-159-0)

Book Code 488—Retail $16.95

THE ULTIMATE GUIDE TO GRAPPLING

by the Editors of Black Belt

Attention, grapplers! This is the book you've been waiting for. From the arenas of ancient Rome to the mixed-martial arts cages of modern Las Vegas, men have always wrestled for dominance. Ground fighting is the cornerstone of combat, and *The Ultimate Guide to Grappling* pays homage to the art with three decades' worth of instructional essays and interviews collected from the archives of *Black Belt*. With more than 30 articles featuring legends like Mike Swain, John Machado, Gokor Chivichyan, Hayward Nishioka, Renzo Gracie, Bart Vale and B.J. Penn, you'll learn the legacy of Greek *pankration*, reality-based ground techniques for police officers and soldiers, the differences between classical *jujutsu* and submission wrestling, and more! Transform your traditional art into a well-rounded and effective self-defense system today! 232 pgs. (ISBN-13: 978-0-89750-160-6)

Book Code 489—Retail $16.95